# RADICALLY CATHOLIC
## In the Age of Francis

*In this fine collection of short essays, Catholic Workers, home-schoolers, environmental activists, scholars, gardeners, bloggers, prolifers, artists, and business owners offer their reflections on how to live as authentically, radically Catholic as they can. This diverse group of writers resist traditional divisions between the Catholic left and the Catholic right. Taking their cue from Pope Francis and the Catholic tradition wholistically conceived, they stand before their readers as pilgrims on a journey and invite others to join them. A great resource for discussion groups, adult education classes, and personal reflection.*

— Julie Hanlon Rubio
  Professor of Christian Ethics, St. Louis University;
  author, *Family Ethics: Practices for Christians*


*How ought Catholics in America think about their relationship to their nation, to liberal democracy, to modernity? The standard answers to that question forged during the JFK/Vatican II years no longer seem adequate. To anyone paying the slightest bit of attention, America, liberalism, and (late) modernity all look and feel different now than they did then. The Catholic writers gathered here realize that. Their suggestions about how Catholics might best orient themselves amidst the disorienting landscape of twenty-first-century America ought to form the basis of a new, more fruitful, and more faithful self-understanding.*

— Jeremy Beer, Ph.D.
  Partner, American Philanthropic, LLC

*Written by Catholic scholars and workers from a striking variety of ages, backgrounds, and perspectives, these essays nevertheless converge to warn us that something is radically wrong with the shape of modern life, and to announce that the way forward is available to the extent that are ready to undertake the radical step of being led by Christ. Imbued with the refreshing spirit of Pope Francis, this book is a testimony that the Catholic Church, in each and every age, has the capacity to return to the wellsprings of the Gospel. A testament of hope for our times.*

—Michael Baxter
Visiting Associate Professor, Department of
Catholic Studies, DePaul University


*Somehow "radical" has come to mean the exact opposite of what it actually means. To be radical is to be rooted, not to be hiving off into deep space in pursuit of some crazy dream unconnected to all that has gone before. To be radically Catholic in the Age of Francis is, therefore, to be rooted in the whole of the Catholic tradition. That is emphatically what Francis is and, O glory hallelujah, it is what this collection of hope-inspiring essays from a group of deeply committed Catholics is as well. It is so heartening to see Catholics who put the Tradition first and refuse to cannibalize it in the service of any of our insane ideologies. May their tribe increase!*

—Mark P. Shea
author, *By What Authority: An Evangelical
Discovers Catholic Tradition*

Radically Catholic in the Age of Francis *presents a diverse range of voices engaging with the central theological and social issues of our era. This is an accessible text that links radical Catholic perspectives to everyday life, revealing the profound link between orthodoxy and orthopraxy advocated by Pope Francis and reflected broadly among the Catholic laity. The volume's four crucial themes—Conscience, Community, City, and Church—cover a range of topics in a manner that is accessible to the non-specialist reader while still valuable for readers with more theological training. This is an important text for anyone seeking to understand the theological and practical nuances of radical Catholic commitments.*

  —Nichole M. Flores, M.Div., Ph.D. Candidate
   Instructor, Department of Theology, Saint Anselm
   College

linocut by Hannah Strauss

# RADICALLY CATHOLIC
## *In the Age of Francis*

An Anthology of Visions for the Future

Edited by Daniel Schwindt

*Solidarity Hall*
*www.solidarityhall.org*

| publisher | Elias Crim |
|---|---|
| editor | Daniel Schwindt |
| contributing editors | Mark Gordon |
| | Susannah Black |
| | Paul Grenier |
| | Grace Potts |
| | Matthew Cooper |
| designer | Paul Bowman |
| cover/frontispiece artist | Hannah Strauss |

The word "solidarity" is a little worn and at times poorly understood, but it refers to something more than a few sporadic acts of generosity.

It presumes the creation of a new mindset which thinks in terms of community and the priority of the life of all over the appropriation of goods by a few.

— *Evangelii Gaudium*

# CONTENTS

## Church

# RADICALLY CATHOLIC
*In the Age of Francis*

# Introduction

Over a year ago, but fresh in memory, I found myself standing with our two teenage daughters on Copacabana Beach in Rio de Janeiro. We were amidst a crowd of over one million people along the gleaming stretch of beachfront. Around us the human ocean was made up of many little groups of people, mostly young, often holding up flags of their various countries—over one hundred, as I later read.

We were there to greet the new Pope, of course. On one level, it was as though the greatest soccer star in world history was about to arrive in the country craziest of all on the subject of soccer. So, superficially speaking, there was an expectant sense of being in the biggest of all possible grandstands before the biggest star arrives for the game.

And yet another dimension of the experience was harder to describe: something about finding oneself in a Latin society, notably with many thousands of Brazilians, Argentinians, Chileans, and Mexicans, celebrating a momentous shift in the Church (and world) history with this new Pope from a Latin country. Possibly, I thought, the new Marian Church desired by the late John Paul II, was arriving.

And do we *norteamericanos* also feel a momentous shift in the Church? The contributors to this collection would seem to say so. At the very least, they are witnesses to the many and various ways our faith seems to be calling us to go deeper in these times.

To possess the hope of becoming more radically Catholic is not to express a political ambition, as all voices here would likely agree. We are not speaking here as "radical Catholics," whatever stereotype that phrase calls to mind. Thus the reader will find in these pages no calls to march on the Pentagon or—for that matter—on the Supreme Court.

Instead the reader will find reflections from twenty-somethings and sixty-somethings, from single women and fathers of large households, from professors and stay-at-home moms, from people of different racial and ethnic backgrounds. Veritably an almost Chaucerian mix of pilgrims, I think.

And yet, however diverse we may be, the cafeteria—the one immortalized in the notorious expression "cafeteria Catholicism"—is now closed. And not just to liberal Catholics at whom the phrase was originally pointed.

For us, the teachings of the current Pope and his two predecessors on the connections between the human person, society and the economy can no longer be submitted to the kind of reductionist hedging with which some American commentators have responded.

More pointedly, it is a remarkable judgment on modern technocracy that the Vatican's views on warfare and economics over the last decade have proven to be much sounder than that of, say, the National Security Council or the Council of Economic Advisors. It is the overconfidence (another name for hubris, of course) of the latter worldview that has led to the destruction of Christianity in the Middle East, something the fiercest of Muslim invaders could never accomplish.

Thus our cultural condition today amounts to love in the ruins, as Walker Percy once titled a novel of his. What do we do now? Pope Francis suggested recently that St. Paul's Letter to the Galatians expresses the new solidarity we seek in a nutshell: "Carry one another's burdens."

Translation for us Americans: Enough with the idea that mailing list politics discharges your obligations to society! No more acquiescing in the recurring emotional blackmail from the political candidate who warns us (as blogger Mark Shea once put it) "vote for me or the baby gets it."

Instead, we could consider, among the over two dozen contributions here, the "Philippian option" (i.e., glory-in-humility), as Julia Smucker counsels. Or the wisdom in developing an "exilic consciousness" (Mark Gordon's topic). Or Elizabeth Stoker Bruenig's invocation of Augustine's law of love. Or Ricardo Simmonds' eloquent call to a *camino*, a literal and spiritual walk that allows creation's beauty to work on our spirits and our understanding.

Or Michel Bauwens' invocation of Church history as anticipating the new movements around restoring the commons and establishing peer-to-peer socioeconomic systems. Or a new sense for our spiritual status as migrants in a migrant Church, as per M T Dávila's fine essay. Or in Nicholas Lund-Molfese's reminder (drawing on his Catholic Worker House experiences) that Christians have *always* been called to live radically, not just when the Pope makes the cover of *Rolling Stone*.

Globally Pope Francis is invoking a reformed liberation theology that leaves behind the statist assumptions of earlier versions. For American Catholics in 2014, striving to live in a radically Catholic way can be a similar kind of liberation. This, we are saying, is where we need to go.

A native Texan, Elias wandered in his youth from classics and medieval Italian at UC Berkeley to a stint in financial journalism around Chicago. He has written for *The American Scholar, The American Conservative, The Washington Times,* and *The Chicago Observer* and is co-author of a textbook on character education. His publishing ventures include something called *The Armchair Historian,* briefly, and Solidarity Hall. He and his family reside in leafy Valparaiso, Indiana.

# CONSCIENCE

# Are Catholic Workers Radically Catholic?

## *A Brief Caution on Self-Labeling and the Nature of Radicalism*

Perhaps I am just a contrarian by disposition, but I find both the Francis mania and the self-ascription of "living radically" difficult to stomach. Christians, when living faithfully to their vocation to be the soul of the world, have been living radically since 33 AD. To live radically, etymologically and actually, is to live by the roots, to draw the substance of your life from the depths, from what is most real and it is in contrast to living in the winds of our own time and place.

Much of Pope Francis' popularity is based on a media story line driven by a few small gestures on his part and by overly dramatic and superficial comparisons with his processor. He has yet to do anything as radical as Pope Benedict did by resigning. Real radicalism tends to get you put on a cross, not on the covers of *Time*, *The Advocate*, and *Rolling Stone*. None of this is Francis' fault. He has genuine gifts for the entire Church, but being a media phenomenon is the opposite of any sense of radicalism worthy of the name.

I am writing this on my 45th birthday, sitting in a military cemetery in the midst of ancient, majestic trees and headstones marking unseen mortal remains. It is a scene which exemplifies radicalism. The trees draw their substance from deep in the ground; their roots unseen and yet most permanent, while the highly visible leaves are gone in a season. The leaves are surrounded by constant change in temperature, conditions and winds while the roots are in contact with the permanence of the earth.

The headstones are white, of uniform dimensions, and in mathematically precise parallel rows. Some are new and others old, but even the new ones are already being worn away by the elements. (In fact, such headstones are replaced *in toto* on a routine basis.) Their showy, bright impermanence is in contrast with what they mark—the final resting place of human remains until the end of the world. The stone is the highly visible marker for the unseen bodies which give the stones their meaning and importance—for a headstone without a body is an empty sign.

## An Example of the Radically Catholic Life in the Person of Peter Maurin

Peter Maurin (1877–1949), co-founder of the Catholic Worker Movement with Dorothy Day, saw the movement as radical, but not in the sense of the political or cultural left or right. As he explained in one of his "Easy Essays,"

A Radical Change

1. The order of the day
   is to talk about the social order.

2. Conservatives would like
   to keep it from changing
   but they don't know how.

3. Liberals try to patch it
   and call it a New Deal.

4. Socialists want a change,
   but a gradual change.

5. Communists want a change,
   an immediate change,
   but a Socialist change.
   …

8. I want a change,
   and a radical change.

9. I want a change
   from an acquisitive society
   to a functional society,
   from a society of go-getters
   to a society of go-givers.

And the place to start building a society of "go-givers" was within your own life by practicing the Works of Mercy which are a practical norm for every community in the Catholic Worker Movement:

The corporal works of mercy:

feeding the hungry
giving drink to the thirsty
clothing the naked
offering hospitality to the homeless
caring for the sick
visiting the imprisoned
burying the dead

The spiritual works of mercy:

admonishing the sinner
instructing the ignorant
counseling the doubtful
comforting the sorrowful
bearing wrongs patiently
forgiving all injuries
praying for the living and the dead

And so we do these things at the Catholic Worker House and Farm in southern Missouri, Trinity Hills. But we try to do them in a personal way. For example, I might ask someone if they want some water and talk with them a bit before we start talking about their situation or filling out forms. In one sense, not very "radical"—but by making a small sacrifice in efficiency for the sake of respecting the person we take a small step toward changing the form of the relationship. As Pope Francis said, "I distrust a charity that costs nothing and does not hurt." Peter Maurin put it this way:

Feeding the Poor at a Sacrifice

1. In the first centuries
   of Christianity
   the hungry were fed
   at a personal sacrifice,
   the naked were clothed
   at a personal sacrifice,
   the homeless were sheltered
   at personal sacrifice.

2. And because the poor
   were fed, clothed and sheltered
   at a personal sacrifice,
   the pagans used to say
   about the Christians
   "See how they love each other."

3. In our own day
   the poor are no longer
   fed, clothed, sheltered
   at a personal sacrifice,
   but at the expense
   of the taxpayers.

4. And because the poor
   are no longer
   fed, clothed and sheltered
   the pagans say about the Christians
   "See how they pass the buck."

Personally practicing the Works of Mercy will entail personal sacrifices, some of which are chosen and some of which come unexpectedly. People have many excuses as to why they need not practice them personally: "I give money to charity" or "what if I get sued" or "what if they take advantage of me." Yes, there may be sacrifice involved and even suffering in loving others. This should not be a shocking idea for Christians who worship a savior who suffered and died for our sake; who told us to take up our cross, daily, and follow him.

One way of practicing a number of the Works of Mercy collectively and simultaneously is "hospitality," which Peter saw as a basic duty of Christians worthy of the name:

The Duty of Hospitality

1.  People who are in need
    and are not afraid to beg
    give to people not in need
    occasion to do good
    for goodness' sake.

2.  Modern society calls the beggar
    bum and panhandler
    and gives him the bum's rush.
    But the Greeks used to say
    that people in need
    are the ambassadors of the gods.

3.  Although you may be called
    bums and panhandlers
    are in fact
    Ambassadors of God.

4.  As God's Ambassadors
    should be given food,
    clothing and shelter
    by those who are able to give it.

5.  Mahometan teachers tell us
    that God commands hospitality,
    and hospitality is still practiced
    in Mahometan countries.

6. But the duty of hospitality
   is neither taught nor practiced
   in Christian countries.

## *Pope Francis and the Gospel of Human Encounter*

Hospitality is the opposite of professionalism. You live with and share in the problems of all in the house. Others have to live with and share in your problems. There is an intimacy to it that some recoil from, a rejection of the person and the body of the poor which Pope Francis has denounced:

> Am I ashamed of the flesh of my brother and sister.... When I give alms, do I drop the coin without touching the hand (of the poor person, beggar)? And if by chance I do touch it, do I immediately withdraw it? When I give alms, do I look into the eyes of my brother, my sister? When I know a person is ill, do I go and visit that person? Do I greet him or her with affection? There's a sign that possibly may help us, it's a question: Am I capable of giving a caress or a hug to the sick, the elderly, the children, or have I lost sight of the meaning of a caress? These hypocrites were unable to give a caress. They had forgotten how to do it.... Don't be ashamed of the flesh of our brother, it's our flesh! We will be judged by the way we behave towards this brother, this sister.

This is the radicalism of Pope Francis, he preaches the Gospel just as Pope Benedict preached it before him. He calls us to live a Christian life and reminds us that God will judge us. The radical truth is to recognize the presence of God, in and with those in need, even when they are unpleasant and ungrateful. The Christian life of a Catholic Worker is found in the living and the suffering and the enduring love.

Finally, there is another risk in calling the Catholic Worker life a radical life, the same one Dorothy Day rejected when someone asked her what she thought about people calling her a saint, "I don't want to be dismissed that easily." Calling it radical can just be another way of dismissing it as an esoteric or unrealistic way for most to live; it is a way of removing the challenge and demeaning the witness. Peter addressed this as well:

Christianity Untried

1. Chesterton says
   "The Christian ideal
   has not been tried
   and found wanting.

2. It has been found difficult
   and left untried."

3. Christianity has not been tried
   because people thought
   it was impractical.

4. And men have tried everything
   except Christianity.

5. And everything
   that men have tried
   has failed.

Nicholas C. Lund-Molfese is husband to Christine and father to their seven children. He serves as the Director of Trinity Hills and Director of the Office for Social Ministry, Evangelization and Formation of the Catholic Diocese of Springfield–Cape Girardeau. The opinions he expresses in this essay are his alone.

# Thinking Well About Things (Other Than Politics)

Two years ago one of our greatest living philosophers, Alasdair MacIntyre, gave a lecture at the University of Notre Dame titled "Catholic instead of what?" MacIntyre always has a way of provoking thought, unsettling our categories, and helping us to understand ourselves and our place in the world. This brilliant lecture was no exception. He began by observing that Catholics have always understood themselves in *contrast* to something else. That is a particularly good starting point for any post-election analysis since Catholics have been increasingly reduced to a political caricature of what they are against (contraception, abortion, redefinition of marriage).

MacIntyre stressed that Catholic Christians have always lived the Christian story in such a way as to unfold its communal learning before the whole world, largely in terms of affirmations and denials. For example, Catholics have always believed and affirmed "that God exists, that the Word was made flesh, that the bread and wine of the Eucharist becomes Christ's body and blood, that the pope and the bishops teach with apostolic authority." But Christians also disbelieve, as often in response to confused internal claims (such as heresies) as to external claims (counter narratives). In each particular time and place, Catholic

Christians have disbelieved anything that provides grounds for rejecting the Catholic faith. That is, MacIntyre stresses, "a reflective Catholic is always a Catholic rather than something else. So Augustine was a Catholic rather than a Manichean; Pascal was a Catholic rather than a skeptic or a Cartesian; Maritain was a Catholic rather than a materialist Bergsonian, etc."

MacIntyre was asking, as he so often does, what it means to be a Catholic Christian in a secular culture. But the context of his comments suggested an even more timely question in the post-election season—one akin to the one he asked in 2004 by reflecting on why he would not be voting—what does it in mean to be a Christian in a liberal democratic culture such as ours? What does it mean to be a Christian in a thoroughly polarized political climate, with a "vulgarized liberalism" on one side, and a "vulgarized conservativism" on the other?

I am prompted to step back from our fractious political climate for a moment to assess: Where are we now? How do Catholics understand themselves in the wake of the last election?

In response to a quite important policy question concerning the HHS mandate, MacIntyre had the good sense to affirm the Bishops in their fight. It is the Bishops, after all, who have led us to ask ourselves (more than anyone else) the question: "Catholic rather than what?" Yet MacIntyre also paused at the dangers implicit in the fight. Is it possible for Catholics to simply become co-opted, subsumed, reducible and redefined by politics? He gave this important caution: "If we are going to think well about politics as Catholics in the United States now, there are a lot of things other than politics that we have to start thinking well about [too]." And I think one of those things that Christians need to think well about is the narrative that shapes how we ourselves think about the shape and scale of our politics. In every age, Christians have found their own narrative to be at odds with other narratives that in some way deform or divide the fundamental unity of Christian faith. At times, Christians can be subtly coerced, often by the psychological force of the general will of the culture they inhabit, to make affirmations and denials that do not flow from their own substantial commitments as Christians, but which mirror affirmations and denials of another narrative.

Currently the literature is awash with accounts of why Christians are more aligned with Republicans, or why Christians are more aligned with Democrats, but I must admit that I find both suggestions equally worrisome. To say that a Christian must be a Republican rather than Democrat, or a Democrat rather than Republican—while having some intellectual cogency with respect to the hierarchy of moral truths under consideration—seems also to be a sign of a very deep confusion worthy of reflection. It should signal a warning: the deepest commitments of Christians are being parceled out for other purposes, deformed and divided for political ends which undermine Christian faith.

For example, Catholics are committed to a strong metaphysical understanding of the justice that is owed to the unborn child. But Catholics are also committed to a strong theological account of the love of neighbor, whose poverty is a constant occasion for the very generosity and friendship that God has given to us in our poverty. Now if the parties are to be believed, this means Catholics should split down the line: half-republican and half-democrat—like some perverse mythological creature. Turns out that, by and large, that split is what happened in the election. That was not a distortion of liberal democracy, but it was a distortion of Christian belief. It was a distortion of the unity of Catholic social teaching. I am not suggesting the Catholics vote in lock-step. Rather, I am suggesting that this division is a sign that Catholic Christians have not been asking—as a group—the "Catholic rather than what?" question. In this sense, the Christian in our current political climate is not really asking the substantial questions concerning Catholic belief. Instead, Catholics are currently faced with a choice which is potentially destructive of Catholic belief: Republican or Democrat? In this post-election season, we have to ask whether our vulgarized modes of partisanship indicate a symptom of a larger problem with the political order we now inhabit, and whether this constitutes a moment for self-understanding of what it means to be Catholic in this political order at this time in history.

Catholics affirm that the state has the authority, within limits, to recognize marriage and to protect people who enter into it; to recognize the sanctity of life, and to do no harm to it; to recognize the dignity of the human person, and therefore ensure an economy in which every person can flourish according to their capacities without being debilitated by poverty. Yet currently, the Catholic is being asked to divide her affirmations and denials more or less equally between political parties that may or may not finally represent these concerns at all. It is like asking King Solomon, or a mother, to tear a child in half.

That means that we are beyond the Churchillian "least bad" problem in choosing between parties. The political culture we inhabit has exceeded that problem. Ours is not only a polarized politics, it is also an excessive politics. It dominates every aspect of life. Political campaigns have learned to carefully cultivate every existing identity for itself, and only for itself. It has come to take over every aspect of life so there is no place where presidential politics is absent. I think *this excessiveness is an enduring aspect of every politics that detaches itself from natural limits,* that consistently refuses to allow space to that which is not politics, that refuses to admit that there is anything prior to politics, that habitually ignores anything which supersedes politics, and which denies anything which is not reducible to politics.

All of this makes my post-election reflections sound like a plea for resistance to political instrumentalism. It is that, but it is also simply a plea for contemplation on those things which are not political, but are nevertheless important to political community. The popular motto of the Catholic resistance movement during WWII, "France, be careful not to lose your soul" is worth recalling to this end. A generation earlier, Charles Péguy, the atheist socialist convert to Catholicism, sought to remind France to attend those things which were preludes to politics: metaphysics, narratives, language, family, friendship and contemplation upon the causes, effects, and ends of our most cherished commitments—our loves and our liberties (to recall St. Augustine). In our post-election reflections, Christians should be the ones asking the really substantial questions. Not the ones asked at our very insubstantial presidential debates, but the questions we would want our children to ask: questions about existence, such as why there is something rather than nothing; about justice, and to whom it is owed; about truth, and making ourselves truthful; about the nature of goodness and how we can be formed in accordance with it. Questions like these are pre-political, but they matter for politics too. If these sorts of question whither, we will get the politics we deserve. Amongst ourselves as well as with others, we must be asking what it means to be a Christian in our excessive, polarized, political order.

At its best, true Christianity has always resisted being instrumentalized by politics — it has always affirmed the legitimate authority of the state, but it has also helped the state to flourish precisely by pointing out its *limits,* and its *disorder.* Sometimes it has done so with martyrs, but usually with a different kind of Christian witness — one which entails discursive reasoning as well as contemplation and prayer, marked by both seriousness and joyfulness about things other than politics but which nevertheless matter for the political health of the places that God has entrusted to us.

Reflective Christians might feel politically homeless in America right now, but if they do, it seems to me that this is an exceedingly good thing because they are finally in a place to ask the more substantial question that MacIntyre suggests that Christians have always asked, not Republican or Democrat, but "Catholic instead of what?"

C. C. Pecknold, Ph.D. is a professor of historical and systematic theology at The Catholic University of America and a member of the *Ethika Politika* editorial board.

# Unlimited: The Cult of the Self

According to the Bible, the ancient Israelites often strayed from worship of God into idolatry. Today, America has done the same—except rather than placing a golden calf upon an altar, we have erected a mirror. And in that mirror, we give glory to our own reflections. Our culture is characterized by a widely-shared form of radical individualism: we have created a *Cult of the Self*.

Before we make a desert of our life, or of our world, we must first have a desert inside us. The Cult of the Self is the force driving the process of desertification in modernity—it creates internal, and then external, wastelands.

The Cult of the Self is based on a mistaken anthropology, a false understanding of the nature of the human person. Its largely negative conception of liberty makes it virtually synonymous with personal license. It is relativistic and nihilistic; materialist and utilitarian. Autonomy—choice—is its highest, and perhaps only, value.

## Life Without Limits

As author Chris Hedges has noted, "[w]e have a right, in the cult of self, to get whatever we desire" or, to use the words of a recent Sprint television commercial, each individual has "a right to be unlimited." Indeed, according to Mark T. Mitchell, in a piece considering the philosophical implications of that same Sprint advertisement, "[i]n our cultural moment, the [very] idea of limits [on the individual] is an offense. Limits suggest that my desires can be thwarted or perhaps even that my desires should be thwarted."

The Cult of the Self misdirects human desire away from God and towards a never-ending series of illusions for us to chase by purchasing consumer goods. It trains us to expect instant gratification. Avarice and greed are transformed from the root of all evil into positive virtues.

The Cult of the Self underpins our mass culture of consumerism and celebrity. It is the common root of the various economic, social, and environmental problems our society faces—from abortion and the decline of the family to growing economic inequality and even global warming. Not surprisingly, the Cult of the Self is inextricably intertwined with our current form of late-modern extractive, exploitative, socially irresponsible capitalism. Indeed, our reckless banks and corporations are in some ways merely reflections of us—as Rev. Daniel M. Bell has observed, they are idealized versions of our modern autonomous Selves "writ large—self-interested and profit-maximizing."

The cultural and economic values of the Cult of the Self are perhaps best illustrated by two popular reality television shows: *Survivor* and *Big Brother*. In both shows, contestants compete for large cash prizes. The so-called "social game" played by the more successful competitors relies on manipulation and lying—predatory behavior is constantly rewarded. Alliances and even friendships are, with few exceptions, mere temporary truces driven by immediate self-interest. Traditional values like honesty, integrity, solidarity, and compassion, are the province of suckers who are quickly voted off. The goal—winning the large cash prize—is used by the contestants as the justification for their behavior towards one another. The moral lesson is clear: the pursuit of wealth excuses just about any action; the end you are chasing justifies the means. And the people around you are objects to be played and manipulated in pursuit of your goal.

These are not just the ethics of reality show contestants, bankers, and venture capitalists; functionally, many of us behave this way in our own professional and personal lives.

## Alone In the Darkness: the Slavery of Selfishness

The promise of radical individualism is that everyone can be clothed in purple, but rather than an emperor's robe, our garments turn out to be beggars' cloaks.

The happiness we are pursuing retreats before us like a mirage.

In the end, the Cult of the Self misdirects desire in ways that can never be satisfied.[1] Humanity is meant to live in community—not as lonely, isolated, autonomous Selves. We are meant to live in communion and fellowship, not seeking to maximize our own self-interests while locked in remorseless competition with others. Far from empowering us, the Cult of the Self renders us helpless. The worship of the Self, the exaltation of personal autonomy, the obsession with being "unlimited," turns out not to be liberating, but instead a penal sentence.[2] It births a terrible emptiness—one we try to avoid facing by distracting ourselves through entertainment, or by escaping from reality through drug or alcohol abuse, or any one of the innumerable other forms of addiction that plague our society.

The lie at the heart of the Cult of the Self, that happiness comes from being an "unlimited" autonomous Self relentlessly pursuing your own self-interest, is perhaps best seen in the context of parenting and marriage. To paraphrase the late Congressman Henry Hyde, every child is an invitation to love! So too is every marriage. Alas, these invitations are frequently left unaccepted in our society. Children, spouses, and families are the ultimate limitations on personal autonomy. They make many demands. They force us to compromise our own wills and desires; they interfere with our career plans, and, at times, with our Saturday evenings.

So, many remain childless; others have children but subcontract raising them. We use them as pawns in divorces. We communicate to them, in innumerable ways, that they are not the priority in our lives. We do the same with our spouses. Marriage, in the Cult of the Self, is more akin to a temporary alliance—a merely contractual, as opposed to

---

[1]  See Isa. 55:2.

[2]  1 Tim. 6:9.

sacramental, relationship. As a result, no-fault divorces are plentiful, even among Christians.

And in the end, we grow old, and we die alone.

The Cult of the Self creates a society of narcissists and sociopaths either incapable of feeling love, empathy, and remorse, or too self-absorbed to care.

Politically, the Cult of the Self is not a phenomenon of the Left or the Right, but rather a shared culture that cuts across the ideological spectrum. Its emergence is not a sudden break with what came before. Instead, it is more akin to a natural development rooted in the political philosophy underpinning our civilization. Today, it drives the social changes bemoaned by conservatives as well as the violence and systemic inequality decried by progressives. It finds expression equally in the cold social Darwinism of Ayn Rand and in the libertine hedonism of the so-called sexual revolution; in the business owner slashing worker wages and benefits or skirting environmental protections to increase his own profits, and in the mother aborting her child because it is inconvenient and an unwelcome interference with her own plans for her future.

Like a massive object in space, the Cult of the Self also exerts a strong gravitational pull that distorts Christian belief and practice in America. This is particularly obvious in the so-called "prosperity gospel" where Christianity is viewed, in the words of Rev. Daniel Bell, Jr., as being "about meeting our wildest consumer dreams." Alternatively, traditional Christian beliefs and teachings—particularly regarding human sexuality and marriage—are stripped away least they impose limitations on the desires of autonomous Selves.

### Christian Resistance and the Refusal of Despair

Is meaningful resistance to the Cult of the Self even possible? Or are we condemned to a series of futile last stands—a long rearguard action inevitably culminating in catastrophe?

The State cannot save us. There is no political solution to the social and spiritual problems posed by the virulent form of radical individualism that characterizes the Cult of the Self. In the words of Dr. Claes G. Ryn:

Traditional civilization is threatened with extinction because pleasing but destructive illusions have become part of the way in which most people view the world and their own lives. The hold on society of those who created and fed these illusions cannot be broken mainly through practical politics....

What is most needed is a reorientation of mind and imagination. The great illusions of our age must be exposed for what they are so that they will start to lose their appeal....

Religion reorients mind and imagination. It, figuratively speaking, gives sight to the blind. And so, the antidote to the toxic Cult of the Self is in the end theological—the solution is faith.

But how can religious faith, particularly orthodox Christian belief, turn back this tide?

The powers arrayed against us seem so strong in comparison to us. How can we possibly prevail over, or even survive, the cultural storm that is breaking?

In the face of these questions, many fall into deep despair, pessimism, and endless hand-wringing.

This is akin to suicide.

The moment we despair, the Cult of the Self has already prevailed, because we have adopted and internalized its definition of power—and it is wrong.

In the eyes of the world, Christ crucified was weak, pitiful and contemptible compared to Pontius Pilate, Caiaphas, and the powers they served and represented. And where are Pilate and Caiaphas now? Where is the Roman Empire or the Sanhedrin? We must look for them amidst the dust and the ruins, because they are all dead and gone. But the fire Christ kindled still burns—it is alive and working in our world today.3 And it will burn on long after the powers of the present—Hollywood, Wall Street, global finance, even the nations have passed into nothingness.

---

3  Luke 12:49; Psalm 104:4.

We may be the sheep amidst the wolves—but beware wolves!

We are not powerless. And to paraphrase Michel Foucault: where there is power, resistance is possible.

Christianity is, and always has been, an act of rebellion against the powers of the world. Christ forces a choice on us: are we with God, or are we against Him? We face this moment of decision on a daily basis, because love "must be pursued chiefly in the ordinary circumstances of life," according to paragraph 38 of *Gaudium et Spes*. And choosing God is a revolutionary act! Of course, by resistance, rebellion, and revolution, we do not mean acts of violence, nor should we conceive of them in political terms. Instead, we should look to the life of Jesus and the early Christian communities—their focus was on making the reign of God a reality in the world, not on overthrowing the existing political order. The violent political rebels, the ones who wanted to make the state the vehicle for enforcing God's will, were the Zealots. Their cause failed, and brought ruin down on Israel.

Christian resistance to the Cult of the Self is not about sweeping gestures on a grand stage, but rather the ordinary choices we make in daily life. Today, we must look for opportunities to live traditional orthodox Christian belief in unorthodox ways. In the end, radical community among believers, built on a firm foundation of solidarity and mutuality, is the only possible solution to the problem of radical individualism run amok. Love—agape—is the answer. Love is, and always has been, our only hope.

In practical terms, we must form and sustain communities of table fellowship, both physical and virtual, conducive to authentic human flourishing—to "love of God [and] love of neighbor"4—that are incubators of virtue. This can take diverse shapes and forms. At a minimum it must involve renouncing any desire or ambition to become wealthy or famous; fostering vertical solidarity between rich and poor as well as horizontal solidarity between consumers and producers; rendering effective assistance to marginalized groups in society such as the poor and immigrants; a shared commitment to traditional values, particu-

---

4  Matt. 22:35–40.

larly with respect to sex and marriage, as well as a recognition of the importance of families and children; opposition to abortion; an emphasis on environmental stewardship and caring for creation; and a commitment to nonviolence. Thankfully, examples of these types of lay Christian communities already exist, such as the Catholic Worker, Focolare and New Monasticism movements.

In addition, personal modesty—in terms of our behavior as consumers—must also be one of our distinguishing characteristics. In our homes, even the pots and pans must be holy!5

The material things we surround ourselves with can be powerful signs of an unclean, disorder soul, and of misdirected desire. In a world awash in the cheap consumerism of the Cult of the Self, our possessions and the value we attach to them speak volumes.

So, amidst the decadence and waste of modernity, we must live modestly. The cars we drive, the houses we live in, the clothes we wear—all should reflect the humility of spirit that distinguishes those living lives of radical discipleship to Christ. By so doing, we demonstrate our rejection of the mores and lifestyles of the Selfies, and become signs of contradiction that can be emulated by others.

Obviously, this has the air of a counter-cultural endeavor to it—however; fundamentally, it is not about dropping out of society, but rather building an alternative parallel culture within the wreck and ruin of modernity—one that can be a teacher to the nations. We are, quite literally, the "[r]epairers of the breach," the "[r]estorer[s] of ruined homesteads."6

It is always easier to lecture than to teach by example, but the latter is far more effective. In an age that recognizes no authority above the Self that can be invoked or appealed to, personal witness becomes of paramount importance. For this reason, we must not merely speak to others of human flourishing; we must show them the garden in bloom. That is, a life more joyful, deeper, richer and fulfilling than any existence imaginable under the slate grey skies of the Cult of the Self.

---

5  Zach. 14:20.

6  Isa. 58:12.

Because, as Karl Rahner, S.J. has observed, a faithful Christian life is not "a duty to be painfully observed," but rather a "glorious liberation ... from the enslavement of mortal fear and frustrating egoism."

The light of our example "must shine before others, that they may see [our] good deeds" and through them, be drawn to God.7 Through our witness, we demonstrate that an alternative exists that can be seen, touched, experience, and most importantly, lived. Thus, we become the mechanism for Ryn's "reorientation of mind and imagination" that exposes the lies, the "great illusions," of the Cult of the Self.

And what they see will be fascinating. It will awaken new hopes, birth new dreams, and many will stream towards it.8

Saying yes to the reign of God, and living it, is never an easy choice. It cuts against comfort and convenience. It is rarely popular. It is often financially, socially, and at times even physically, dangerous. As Chris Hedges, writing about the German resistance to the Nazi's, has observed, "[t]hose rare individuals who have the moral and physical courage to resist must accept that they will be pariahs." Here, our very existence is simultaneously an example, an invitation, and a stinging rebuke to the rest of the world. And because of the latter, we will be targets of scorn, derision, and abuse.9

In times such as ours, it takes courage to love.

---

7  Matt. 5:14–16.

8  Isa. 2:2.

9  Isa. 58:15.

Michael Stafford is a 2003 graduate of Duke University School of Law and a former Republican Party officer. He works as an attorney in Wilmington, Delaware and writes a syndicated op-ed column. His writing has been featured on the Australian Broadcasting Corporation's Religion and Ethics portal, MSNBC, *ResPublica,* and *FrumForum.*

# Christian Dialectic and the Franciscan Church

This "Age of Francis" is at once as illuminating as it is obscure. The radical sense of Catholicism it incites is as varied as it is powerful. Two things stand out to me as hallmarks of this era, and of the intelligent, timely response we're called to make as Christians living in it. The first has to do with an emerging clarity concerning the immediate, personal meaning of the word "Catholicism;" the second with the application of that meaning to the world around us.

It may seem strange that on one hand Catholicism has never been more acceptable than it is today. Its concern for the poor and marginalized, represented in the apostolate of Pope Francis, shares a space with the most widely accepted and popular American social ideals. Of course, as we're coming to find out, it's a bit of a linguistic trick: while Franciscan Catholicism is popularly palatable, to "be Catholic" is as unintelligible and only moderately satisfying as ever. The Western world continues its field day with our antiquated doctrines and beliefs, and our best responses continue to remain unimpressive.

Lest we forget, though, we've played this trick on ourselves. The appearance of Catholicism's widespread acceptance is connected intimately to its structure: it's an *ism* word, and it fits well within our mostly unimaginative framework of binary, up-down, left-right thinking. The Catholicism we as Westerners fight vigorously to defend is often inextricably tied to other isms which we admire, and which end up permeating its requisite self-extended boundaries. Most importantly, Catholicism is today universally *disconnected* from the complete cultural context, whereby it became comprehensive and self-extended in the first place. Put differently, it's not wrong that Catholicism is an *ism;* but it is wrong—if the deposit of faith is truth—to act as though it is but one among many.

The result of this *disconnect*—and I suspect part of the motivation for this book—is a crisis among (at least) contemporary Western Catholics on the very content of their shared identity. The "Age of Francis" illuminates because it reminds us to answer the fundamental questions: "Who do I say that Christ is? And what do I believe about his Church?" It obscures because it does not contain a clear and distinct answer; or better, it suggests that an answer isn't the sort of thing that can be clear and distinct at all.

The crux of this dilemma predictably plays out in a sharply divided response to socio-political problems—we might even call them persecutions. One advocates staking our Christian claim in the "public square" and proclaiming loudly our belief in the truth for all to hear. It involves little imagination on the part of truth seeking, yet an exorbitant amount on the part of economic and political theory. In a word, it focuses primarily on defining and defending the limits of the public square, and only secondarily on defining and defending the limits of the fullness of truth. An alternate response advocates pushing boundaries on the meaning of truth, and thinking less about the medium by which it is conveyed. Each response is tactical, yet each is not equally appropriate.

There is another consideration, too, one that relates to "ages" of the Church in general, which further measures our polarized reactions to cultural and intellectual persecution. Simply put, it's the idea that Plato got something very right in his response to the pre-Socratics—the atomists and elementalists—and that this lesson is as important today as ever. The absolutism of Democritus is not disconnected from the "modern turn," both in physical and moral senses. The age of early Greek "philoso-physics," with its emphasis on linear motion and plenitude, matches in many ways the progression of ideologies after Descartes. There are variances in either case: for example, Heraclitus comes close to a sort of "participation" schema of *logos*, but the presentation of dogma itself requires too much rigidity to break the absolutist mold.

The brilliance of Plato, and one that Western Christians must rediscover, is the unique power of dialectic[1] to transform otherwise inscrutable phenomena into intelligible points of possible agreement. At the risk of becoming ironically pedantic, it's dialectic that opens doors for the authentic presentation of dogma. This is true on the macro level: consider Aristotle's *Metaphysics* which benefitted immensely from Plato's refutation of the philosophical status quo. It's also true on the micro level: for example, having neighbors for dinner, showing the guts of a Christian family, and learning happily that morals and affections you've never spoken of are on their hearts, too.

The resuscitation of dialectic is, for many of us, corollary to our experience of a broken social response to the call of the Gospel. For this reason, and since it has the tendency to cause seismic shifts, dialectic is the ultimate feature of our present time. As some have said, the "Age of Francis" is distinctly post-modern because it engages and challenges the hegemony of modernity; and dialectic—rightly exercised—demands answers. To put this in a slightly different light, dialectic is the mode of evangelization in which the mature Christian finds himself, and with which he must be content at least for a while. (The comparison to early Roman Christianity is fitting in this regard, although many other ages like this have come and passed as well. A counterpoint would be the dogmatic mode of evangelization advanced to great benefit in the age of scholasticism.)

Apart from "finality," there is another good reason to emphasize the fittingness of evangelizing through dialectic: namely, since it is the primary mode of thinking almost across the board in the very areas where the truth of the Gospel is most required. A recent surge of inter-

---

[1] A method of argumentation in which participants question each other's premises, attempting to draw out contradictions and discover the truth through a dialogue of back-and-forth, reasoned cross-examination.

est in the philosophy of Marx, for example, shows this in an unalloyed way. The same thing is true, although more obscured, in the general, all-consuming cultural preference for equality. Yet while dialectic has emerged as the prominent trend, its raw materials are lacking. This produces at best an emphasis on resolution, but short of a capacity for just what is being resolved, and whither. "One love" is Heraclitus reloaded.

If the "Age of Francis" is enlightened, it is so just in case it allows us to practice Christian dialectic more fruitfully. Here, I think, we ought to be cautiously optimistic. So far in the Franciscan papacy we have seen daily emphasis laid on the art of the encounter; we have also witnessed any number of painful encroachments into enemy territory—into the language and devices of acultural and emotivist worldviews. All of this has placed us on high alert, but for what reason? I dare say that the things we fear to lose the most—the intelligibility of the Church's teaching on the dignity of family and human life, the priority of the common good, even the beauty of the liturgy—are the very things that demand a "Platonic turn," one that invariably reaches into the muck of incomplete ideas, and with a bit of virtuous unknowing produces a glimpse of goodness worthy of deep affection.

As it happens, if all of this is correct, the last thing we can do is judge the "Age of Francis" as a success or failure. We are stuck—maybe for the best, and in real Franciscan form—in a moment of intuition. Here, our alternatives are somewhat limited, although not necessarily bad. We are still free to pursue truth, to evangelize and to teach about Christ on the shoulders of the great intellectual and spiritual tradition of the Church. Yet our freedom is mostly an intensive one: less the social and cultural climate to extend the Church laterally, as in Early or High Middle Ages, our option is to permeate deeply the thin relationships we still do possess.

Andrew M. Haines is a Ph.D. candidate in the School of Philosophy at The Catholic University of America. He is chief technology officer at Fiat Insight, a DC-based web strategy firm that he co-founded. He lives in Northern Virginia with his wife, Kathleen, and their three children.

# Babylon's Falling: Recovering an Exilic Christian Consciousness

## The Philosophical Empire of the West

*Oh, Jesus, tell you once before*
*Babylon's falling to rise no more*
*O go in peace an' sin no more*
*Babylon's falling to rise no more* [1]

In his 1943 address to the graduating class of Harvard College, Winston Churchill famously declared, "The empires of the future are the empires of the mind." He was as wrong as he was right. All empires—past, present, and future—are essentially empires of the mind because they rest on the normative power of ideas: the divine mediation of pharaoh, emperor, or king; romanitas; the white man's burden; blood and soil; the dictatorship of the proletariat; the "blessings" of liberty. Sir Edward Taylor, the father of social anthropology, wrote, "culture, or civilization, taken in its broad, ethnographic sense, is that complex whole which includes

---

[1] "Babylon's Falling," negro spiritual

knowledge, belief, art, morals, law, custom, and any other capabilities and habits acquired by man as a member of society." At the heart of every culture is its 'cult,' a set of ideas and practices, often religious or at least possessing profound religious implications, that achieves its apotheosis in the flowering of empire.

Given this, it is not at all a stretch to say that Catholics in the post-Christian West find ourselves as captives and strangers in a new empire of the mind, the Empire of Man, which is marked by incredible technological achievement and vast material wealth, but at the heart of which lies a cult that is fundamentally at odds with the Christian understanding of man. Pope Paul VI neatly defined that cultic heart in his 1971 apostolic letter marking the 80th anniversary of Pope Leo XIII's encyclical, *Rerum Novarum.* "At the very root of philosophical liberalism," the Pope wrote, "is an erroneous affirmation of the autonomy of the individual in his activity, his motivation and the exercise of his liberty."

This identification of the Empire of Man's faulty philosophical basis should have served as an invitation to Catholics to engage in a wholesale re-examination of their relationship to the liberal order. Yet, in what will someday be recognized as a demonstration of appalling syncretic dissonance, many Catholics burrowed deeper into the bosom of that empire at the very time the Holy Father published this and other letters, notably *Humanae Vitae.* In the central areas of marriage, sexual ethics, economics, and culture, Catholic imperial viziers wrote treatises, organized conferences, founded organizations and journals, introduced legislation, and captured institutions, all with the intent of defending the Empire of Man and its cultic heart against the backwardness of Catholic teaching. These viziers—on the left and right—have steadily extended the suzerainty of the Empire of Man to this day, with the result that Catholics in the United States think and behave like any other imperial subjects.

In charity, many of the deformations of character and belief that resulted from the empire's rapid expansion since 1970 were not evident in the early years (though they were all predicted, often with stunning accuracy). But today there is no mistaking the effects of the Empire of Man's "erroneous affirmation." Even a cursory examination of the contemporary moral landscape authenticates the writer Christopher Ferrara's assertion that "Liberalism is in thought (or philosophy), rationalism; in politics, secularism; in economics, greed; and in religion, indifferentism."

In the summer of 2014, the Synod of Bishops published a working document—titled, "The Pastoral Challenges of the Family in the Context of Evangelization"—in preparation for an Extraordinary General Assembly of bishops planned for that autumn. That assembly's task was, in part, to examine this question: Why do Catholics routinely ignore Church teaching on marriage, sexuality and family life?

In the section of the working document that summarized responses to a Vatican questionnaire on this question, the following were proffered by episcopal conferences around the world as answers: "pervasive and invasive new technologies; the influence of the mass media; the hedonistic culture; relativism; materialism; individualism; the growing secularism; the prevalence of ideas that lead to an excessive, selfish liberalization of morals; the fragility of interpersonal relationships; a culture which rejects making permanent choices, because it is conditioned by uncertainty and transiency, a veritable 'liquid society' and one with a 'throw away' mentality and one seeking 'immediate gratification'; and, finally, values reinforced by the so-called 'culture of waste' and a 'culture of the moment....'"

I'm not aware of a better list of the existential waste products generated by the Empire of Man. To it we might add the worship of the state, on the left, and the nation, on the right. The Goddess of Liberty, the 'New Colossus' lifts her lamp beside the golden door, but in its reflected glow we see a darkness descending that was hinted at by the poet Leonard Cohen:

> Things are going to slide, slide in all directions
> Won't be nothing you can measure anymore.
> The blizzard of the world has crossed the threshold
> And has overturned the order of the soul.
> When they said REPENT REPENT
> I wonder what they meant...
> I've seen the future, baby:
> It is murder.

## The Perpetual Fall of the Empire of Man

Babylon—or Rome, if you prefer—is indeed falling. But then, Babylon is always falling, which is to say that there has always been a Babylon and the Christian people have always been exiles within it. I once attended a talk by Fr. Benedict Groeschel, CFR, in which he made the case that St. Augustine is the most important Christian figure for our time. It might seem strange, Fr. Benedict allowed, to talk about a Fifth Century bishop in this way, even one whose work is so central to Western civilization. But Augustine lived at a time very much like our own: the classical, pagan world he inhabited was collapsing and beyond it laid a darkness that would be broken only—and only incompletely— by the emergence of Christendom. In our time, the last echo of that imperfectly realized Christian civilization is like background radiation in the cosmos, detectable only by experts with finely tuned instruments and a passion for discovery.

Christendom's successor, the Empire of Man, now stands at the brink of its own denouement, the result of its internal contradictions: ordered liberty collapsing into disordered license, wealth dissolving into the poverty of conscience, the exaltation of reason yielding vast ignorance, neutrality toward religion devolving into hostility toward all truth-claims, democracy perverted by corporate elites, the vision of peaceful cooperation among nations betrayed by militarism. Those who built the Empire of Man thought they could make reason alone the cornerstone of their project. They denied any *telos* beyond "the pursuit of happiness," and sundered the intimate connections between tradition and community. They made "liberty" their god, but at the expense of virtue, the one thing that could sustain it. As Eliot observed,

> They constantly try to escape
> From the darkness outside and within
> By dreaming of systems so perfect
> That no one will need to be good.
> But the man that is will shadow
> The man that pretends to be.

The man that pretends to be now stares into an abyss, but he can't see it. Nor can he hear the man that is whispering in his ear, calling him back to virtue, tradition and community. He has, in the words of Jeremiah, *eyes that cannot see, ears that cannot hear.* The Empire of Man is all he's ever known, and the strange babbling of the Christian remnant around him merely deepens his confusion and stokes his anger. Before him, like Augustine, lies a period of chaotic darkness, made, to quote Churchill again, "more sinister, and perhaps more protracted, by the lights of perverted science." What follows that, who can know?

Theoreticians of collapse have abounded during the past twenty-five years. Some can be easily dismissed, but others have important things to say about how civilizations decline and ultimately fall apart. They include the evolutionary biologist Jared Diamond, author of *Collapse: How Societies Choose to Fail or Succeed;* the systems theorist Thomas Homer-Dixon, author of *The Upside of Down: Catastrophe, Creativity, and the Renewal of Civilization;* and the anthropologist Joseph Tainter, author of *The Collapse of Complex Societies.*

Each of these thinkers identifies hyper-complexity as the prime driver of social collapse; but their work is largely confined to exploring the environmental and economic pressures that contribute to a fatal loss of social resilience. Unfortunately, none of them explores the contributions of moral hyper-complexity, especially in a society where atomized individuals, detached from tradition and community, are encouraged to define, in the words of Justice Anthony Kennedy, "one's own concept of existence, of meaning, of the universe, and of the mystery of human life." Such a society—indeed, such a civilization—is infinitely more complex and therefore far more susceptible to shocks than one in which there is general agreement about ethics, morality, the meaning of life, and the purposes of community. The inability of even leading social scientists to see that is further evidence that the Empire of Man is built on an "erroneous affirmation."

### Directions and Possibilities for a Catholic Recovery

What's a Catholic Christian to do?

First, be a Catholic, in every sense of the word, which is a radical and even revolutionary way of life; and not just in the Empire of Man but also within the Church herself! A radical Catholic will reject the syncretism of party labels, political allegiances, secular ideologies, and even attachments to nation. Our Church today is weighed down with Catholics who view the faith through the lens of the culture rather than the other way around. A radical Catholic will be a Christian first, subjecting every truth-claim, worldview and party platform to the authentic magisterial teaching of the Church. He or she will be a student of the teaching of the Church, including her social doctrine, which frustrates and confounds the contented subjects of the Empire of Man.

Second, cultivate the consciousness of a people in exile, pilgrims in an alien land. The Kingdom of God is our true home and destiny, and while we sojourn here below the Church is our country. Therefore, our communion extends beyond artificial divisions, including national borders, to encompass all the baptized, wherever they may be. That was the perspective of St. Augustine, who wrote in *The City of God:*

> But, as the earthly city has had some philosophers whose doctrine is condemned by the divine teaching, and who, being deceived either by their own conjectures or by demons, supposed that many gods must be invited to take an interest in human affairs, and assigned to each a separate function and a separate department... and as the celestial city, on the other hand, knew that one God only was to be worshipped, and that to Him alone was due that service which the Greeks call *latreia,* and which can be given only to a god, it has come to pass that the two cities could not have common laws of religion, and that the heavenly city has been compelled in this matter to dissent, and to become obnoxious to those who think differently, and to stand the brunt of their anger and hatred and persecutions, except in so far as the minds of their enemies have been alarmed by the multitude of the Christians and quelled by the manifest protection of God accorded to them. This heavenly city, then, while it sojourns on earth, calls citizens out of all nations, and gathers together a society of pilgrims of all languages.

Third, practice the corporal and spiritual works of mercy with zeal: Feed the hungry, give drink the thirsty, clothe the naked, give shelter to the homeless, care for the sick, visit the imprisoned, bury the dead, admonish sinners, instruct the ignorant, counsel the doubting, give comfort to the sorrowful, bear wrongs patiently, forgive all injuries, and pray for the living and dead, including your enemies. This is a radical program for life, what Peter Maurin called "the dynamite of the Church." This is the heart of discipleship, inspired by the Cross, fueled by the Sacraments and empowered by the Holy Spirit.

Last, be prepared for ridicule and persecution, not just from those we already offend—"liberals," "right-wingers"—but also from everyone, on all sides. A Christian who has never been ridiculed or persecuted, especially by those he considers his friends, has good reason to wonder what's wrong with his faith. And a Christian who constructs his life in order to avoid ridicule and persecution isn't worthy of the name. Too many of us have become imperial subjects, happy to get along by going along. Pope Francis is calling us to something higher and far more risky. He's asking us to recover the radical perspective of St. Peter, who wrote "Beloved, do not be surprised that a trial by fire is occurring among you, as if something strange were happening to you. But rejoice to the extent that you share in the sufferings of Christ, so that when his glory is revealed you may also rejoice exultantly. If you are insulted for the name of Christ, blessed are you, for the Spirit of glory and of God rests upon you" (1 Peter 4:12).

> After this I saw another angel coming down from heaven,
> having great authority, and the earth became illumined by
> his splendor. He cried out in a mighty voice:
>
> "Fallen, fallen is Babylon the great.
> She has become a haunt for demons.
> She is a cage for every unclean spirit,
> a cage for every unclean bird and disgusting beast ...
> Then I heard another voice from heaven say:
> 'Depart from her,' my people,
> so as not to take part in her sins
> and receive a share in her plagues ...
> for her sins are piled up to the sky,
> and God remembers her crimes."
>
> (Revelation 18:1–5)

Mark Gordon is a writer and business owner. He also serves as president of both the Society of St. Vincent de Paul, Diocese of Providence, and a local homeless shelter and soup kitchen. Mark is the author of the recent book *Forty Days, Forty Graces: Essays By a Grateful Pilgrim.*

# Could the Preferential Option for the Poor End the Abortion Wars?

## The Unacknowledged Consensus

In the midst of what has become a prohibitively risky topic to touch, abortion remains uncontroversial in at least one respect: No one wants to have one. There is no one advocating for or against legal abortion that wants women to routinely get abortions. Both sides would like to see abortion rates decrease and even someday become obsolete. That this radical consensus has been so callously overlooked in public discourse is a sign of the ideological blindness of the discussion.

There are a number of immediate, but predictable, objections from either side that would quarrel with, and ultimately reject, these opening remarks. In the extreme, the positions would be as follows: Those opposed to legal abortion will claim that abortion advocates are actually genocidal social engineers who want to casually kill babies, especially the poor and disenfranchised. Those who support legal abortion will claim that abortion abolitionists are sick misanthropes who would cause an increase of illegal back-alley abortions and paying no attention to the fate of the child after birth, especially if that child is a female.

Each side has their penny's worth of truth, but both miss the opportunity to acknowledge that people of goodwill, especially people who love their daughters and sisters, do not want to be faced by the possibility of having an abortion in the first place.

No one wants to have an abortion. There is no need for medical or metaphysical consensus to understand this. The option of abortion only becomes the case in limited and often torturously difficult cases. The key, then, is a matter of how to reduce the possibility for any kind of abortion to even become a relevant option—this about the conditions that create the possibility of abortion, legal or illegal.

A question, then, emerges: How do those who oppose *and* support legal abortion work together to bring the material conditions for the possibility of the great abortion debate to an end?

In case anyone is moved to misunderstand, I do not see this as a "middle way," a moderate or conciliatory strategy. Quite the opposite: This is to ask how we might bring to a lasting and holistic end the material, social, economic, spiritual, and political conditions that enable the medical procedure of abortion. Full stop. This is the sort of radical futurism that present attitudes seem to lack, regardless of their objective. Sure, there is a lot of work to do and there is nothing easy about imagining a world in which it is never necessary, and therefore impossible, to consider having an abortion, but, lacking this radical vision and hope, the exercise becomes little more than a series of defensive postures, hedging bets with inevitable despair.

Surely, as I have said already and will repeat once more, there is no one who wants to keep abortion legal just for the hell of it. There are no serious recreational opinions about abortion. It is, at the very least, as serious as a heart attack. The Clintonian "pro-choice"[1] anthem makes no issue of the fact that this should ideally be safe, legal and, *rare.* Even the more radical approaches that oppose the language of "rare" do not say the converse. No one argues that abortions should be frequent. This

---

[1] I use these the expressions "pro-choice" and "pro-life" because these are each group's preferred nomenclature, not because I find the terms useful. There is merit in calling a group of people the name they prefer to go by, but it would be a mistake to think much more than that in this instance.

is where the "pro-life" response should find solidarity instead of rancor and ask, "How rare is rare?" To repeat the question another way, "How can we make abortion as rare as possible?" These are radical, not moderate, questions.

The highest volume of activist opinion about abortion tends to see it as a primarily juridical and legislative affair. Support and opposition of abortion usually boils down to the question of whether abortion *laws* should remain, be extended, or be prohibited. This approach is short-sighted. It is not hard to see that there is an array of factors that con-tribute to the event of abortion and most of them are out of the reach of the narrow, linear scope of what laws concerning abortion should be about.

## Prohibition Is Not Abolition

In other words, it is not necessarily the case that the way to abolish something is to change the relevant laws. Prohibition is not the same thing as abolition. In fact, it is entirely possible, and highly probable when we study the historical record, that legal changes could be ineffec-tive or even counterproductive. All predictions of this sort are unrelia-ble, but the present fact that the legally-focused politics of abortion has reached an unproductive climax is fairly obvious to anyone who spends time engaging (or even avoiding) the topic. To "win" the courts, the legislative session, or even the fickle polls of public opinion, does not necessarily correlate to a lasting victory for either side.

Before suggesting an alternative, let us consider two more objec-tions. On either side there are essential positions, rooted in very real truths, that create inflexible reactions to suggestions that do not explic-itly share and pay homage to their sacred foundations. Both positions would scoff the "absence of the desire to have an abortion" and point to more immediate realities that, on their view, take priority.

For the "pro-choice" side, there is a view that abortion is beyond the scope of desire because it is a right. On this view it is part of the right to autonomy (i.e., the right for a person to decide and choose how to live) necessary to safeguard the ability for women to live and flourish. This view is based in the unobjectionable and fundamental reality that women are the moral equivalent of men—and have historically been harmed by being treated otherwise—and therefore ought to have control over their body in the same proportion as men. The sins against this doctrine are clear, grave, and cut deep; to ignore or overlook the harms that justify this view is callous and inhumane. To prohibit abortion, on this view, then, is to deny women a fundamental right and add to the long record of patriarchal abuse. When cases that threaten the life of the mother, and also the repugnance of rape or incest, are added, the burdens and blows are soul crushing.

For the "pro-life" side, there is another view that abortion is not about desire because it is tantamount to killing and nothing more or less. This logic is rooted in the developmental result of pregnancy: Childbirth. To terminate a viable pregnancy through medical means, then, is to end the life of a child and, in turn, to deny that child its right to live. This approach measures out "life" in different ways, from fetus viability (i.e., the ability of an unborn infant to survive outside the womb) to the more expansive view that life begins at conception. Regardless of the calculus, however, the catalog of offenses against children is also long and cries out for justice. To allow legal abortion, on this view, would endorse an irreversible offense against children that shares many of the traits of murder (despite there being very few who think that women who have abortions should actually be tried for murder). When the selection of sex and ability becomes a part of the equation, as it has in China and India (and even New York), the harms are compacted and fester.

There are significant problems with each of theses views, despite their portion of the truth. For one, each approach divides the material entities of pregnancy, or at least heavily favors one against the other, even to the point of annihilation. To reduce pregnancy to a binary of mutually exclusive options is not only crass, it also has a distinctly martial, masculine severity. A perhaps greater problem is temporal: Both of these views focus on the time of "pregnancy" as the only time relevant to abortion. This limits the realm of possibility and explains why, for both sides, legal battles are the preferred terrain. By expanding or restricting laws that focus on abortion within the period of pregnancy, favoring one material entity at the expense of the other, each side thinks it is winning or losing the day.

There is also a more modest issue with the view that abortion is either a women's right or tantamount to murder: Both of these supposedly "essential" positions are highly contingent. The "right" to have an abortion presupposes its necessity. "Murder" is not as cut and dry as many would have it. Even in the cases of adults killing adults, there are variable *degrees* of murder, motives and contexts that can vastly effect and change the situation and culpability. Consider the case of war: Here we find people legally authorized and even compelled to kill other people. Innocent women and children are often casualties. What do we make of this? At the very least it is not inconceivable to entertain the idea that there is precedent for the legal right to kill, with murderous consequences. As menacing as that may sound, the point is not to provoke scandal. It is simply to show that there are situations that lack the popular controversy of abortion that make far greater demands on our moral imagination.

Objections aside, there are also valuable demands placed upon anyone seeking to offer a different approach to abortion by both sides. We must not forget or erode the place of the women, individually and as a whole, nor can we do the same to children. When one side tries to reject the other using its point of emphasis (e.g., saying that woman's right trumps any consideration whatsoever of a child, or that an infant's potential life trumps any consideration whatsoever of its mother), violence ensues in the discourse itself. To be clear, the ultimate failure of "pro-choice" and "pro-life" approaches is this: They reduce into a perverse form of discursive violence that pits margin against margin, woman against child, weak against the weak. That men escape this clash is significant and instructive to the deeply patriarchal tenor of the present discussion. Why is it the case that women and children are forced to compete for rights and life, while men observe and legislate the battle, from a safe (strategic?) distance?

## The Preferential Option for the Poor, for the Mother, and for the Child

It is here where the preferential option for the poor makes a direct and unsophisticated entrance. Catholic Social Teaching has developed a notion called "the preferential option for the poor and vulnerable" that has also been too narrowly understood in terms of its range and potential. This idea is mostly applied to questions of political economy, but I believe it has wider and more varied uses, including abortion. This option for the poor is *preferential* because it harkens back to the idea as old as the Old Testament: A society has a unique responsibility to care for the weak, the oppressed, the marginalized, the vulnerable. The most recognizable characters of the litany of the oppressed have traditionally been the widow and the orphan. Women and children have a special place as "the poor." (As do the elderly, the immigrant, and others.)

Without quoting ecclesial documents or studying theological doctrine, everyday people can understand that a beautiful society is one in which women and children are given preferential treatment. Why? For a variety of reasons, but one of them is restorative and even penitential: The modern world is one that, by the grace and mercy of God, has come to recognize the gross inequalities between men and women and adults and children, resulting in despicable abuses. Abortion activists, for and against, often refer to this, but they do so selectively.

As I have shown, the present state of "pro-choicer" against "prolifer" violates the preferential option for the poor in an extreme way: It pits the widow against the orphan, the woman against the child, and vice-versa. Regardless of who wins this battle, the root causes will remain untouched. This would be to win at a total cost, to sin against hope.

I am personally not surprised or even offended that so many of my brother and sisters see abortion as a necessary and even salutary option to protect women from abuse and oppression. Nothing will change this position unless women no longer feel the need to be protected from abuse and oppression, and that ought to be the place where the real work begins. I understand the passion of my friends who cannot imagine abortion as anything of that sort, but I am confused as to why they don't try to pull the weed from the roots, and risk everything to provide for the needs of women and children before, during, and after pregnancy. Crisis pregnancy centers are not negligible, but more comprehensive and structural social reform is needed.

The preferential option for the poor offers a way to do more than change laws or popular opinion, it offers a way out of war and into peace, a feminine and childlike way, where the oppressed are not merely treated as objects of favor, but where they are seen as the faces of Christ. The link between abortion and the poor could not be stronger and it gathers its most theological image in the relationship between the child Jesus and his mother, Mary. We must imitate Christ and love (and obey) our mothers, all of them. Until we do this, there will be no easy or lasting consolation.

 Sam Rocha is assistant professor of philosophy of education at the University of British Columbia, a blogger at the *Patheos* Catholic channel, and a soul musician. His debut LP is an Augustinian soul album titled, *Late to Love.*

# COMMUNITY

# Kinship With the Poor

*Francis is challenging 21st Century Catholics to break beyond the limits of "serving" the poor. We must remember them as our friends.*

For decades now, American Catholics have been being told that they should care for the poor. Many of us descendants of immigrants who themselves weathered great poverty, we try to balance a sense of guilt and responsibility toward the poor with our pursuit of greater education and influence. A small, dedicated minority of Christians work daily with the poor, intimately familiar with the nuances of dialoging the Gospel with life. The rest of us tidily summarize our sense of social responsibility with the letters we write our congressmen in defense of the right to life, the sanctity of marriage, and religious freedom. Donations and volunteer hours are slated in alongside work, dance recitals, hair appointments, and vacations as normal. The potential agape has in transforming our daily priorities thus largely remains untapped in modern American Catholicism. The energy we have to "act justly and to love mercy"[1]

---

[1] Micah 6:8

seems to be expended by the time our SUV's or minivans make it through the parking lot after Sunday Mass.

Far beyond the American way of guilting, incentivizing, or competitivizing what we can do for the poor, Pope Francis emphasizes what they can do for us. "Men of good will," he says, "must work, each with his own strengths and expertise, to ensure that love for others increases until it is equal and possibly exceeds love for oneself."[2] The healing of the world's woundedness, in other words, will come about not through non-profit outreach, legislative action, or even public education. Rather through a series of amazingly personal undertakings by each of us.

*Focus not on knowing about poverty, but on experiencing poverty and knowing the poor.*

> This is why I want a Church which is poor and for the poor. They have much to teach us.... In their difficulties they know the suffering Christ. We need to let ourselves be evangelized by them. (*Evangelii Gaudium*, 198)

Think how much better the world would be if all the people talking about poverty and hunger were actually hungry and poor. There are currently over 2.1 million tax exempt/nonprofit organizations in our country, with assets of over $7 trillion and income of over $3 trillion![3] But unless we are especially mindful about practicing subsidiarity, involving those most affected by the issue in its solution, those who live the messiest of life's circumstances are the least likely to be heard in the conversations about them.

This became a stark realization for me a little over a year ago, after moving abruptly from a Catholic Worker community. Exhausted and alone, I was completely confounded with how to incorporate voluntary poverty and a desire to be available to the weak and unseen with the

---

[2] Scalfari, Eugenio. "How the Church will Change." *Repubblica*, October 13, 2013.

[3] http://www.taxexemptworld.com

pursuit of stability in life—a stability I desperately needed to start finding. An old friend had provided me with a calm, judgment-free space in her basement to stay for however long I needed. I had no means of transportation, no real income, and was in the throes of a deep depression. While I had, for years, p ided myself on being an advocate for the working poor, I had not, since youth, counted myself as one of them.

Once I finally got a car, I needed a job. I leveraged the three years I spent studying in Italy to get a waitressing job at an Italian restaurant. There were multiple days I ate all three meals in my car, working up to four double-shifts a week. On Tuesdays I rushed to the Veterans Hospital for therapy directly after work, noticing the stares in the lobby as the restaurant stench that clang to my uniform filled the air around us. I learned more about poverty during those months of limbo than I had in any of my time studying development and social change in college, organizing international symposiums on markets, culture and ethics in Rome, or volunteering for the "under-served" in urban epicenters.

Dorothy Day once said, "We need always to be thinking and writing about poverty, for if we are not among its victims its reality fades from us. We must talk about poverty, because people insulated by their own comfort lose sight of it."4 And this is what has happened to most Americans in their attitude toward the poor.

But God wants to replace our hearts of stone with human hearts. Encountering the poor proves the tenuousness of what we've latched onto as our identity if our identity is anything more or less than Christ alone. Anyone who's been, or sat with, a convict, addict, immigrant, child suffering the loss of a parent, cancer patient, or single mother knows this tenuousness. It is the kind that strips away the layers of distinction and membership we use throughout the rest of the day to get things done or claim our plot. And we just sit there. Sit in the ambiguity of being tossed from place to place; being unable to communicate or being willfully ignored; feeling an insidious skepticism toward life. It leaves little more than two raw and vulnerable people, trying to understand their experience. This is where Jesus is found. To join in union with the poor, to see the merit of poverty, and to become poor oneself

---

4 Day, Dorothy. *Loaves and Fishes.* 1st ed. New York: Harper & Row, 1963.

means to seek out opportunities to shed the identity we've built for ourselves that has made us austere and certain, and become, like Christ, more approachable, open, and grateful.

*Look not for big, glossy moments of change, but for opportunities to join in the rawness of everyday life.*

> It is essential to draw near to new forms of poverty and vulnerability, in which we are called to recognize the suffering Christ, even if this appears to bring us no tangible and immediate benefits. I think of the homeless, the addicted, refugees, indigenous peoples, the elderly who are increasingly isolated and abandoned, and many others. (*Evangelii Gaudium*, 210)

I met Jeneth in a big moment. She had just been released from prison on house arrest after twenty years, and my work in jail ministry for the diocese of the fourteen counties of Northeast Indiana had just begun. I would feverishly scribble down the stories she shared each time we met. Her path from drugs and homicides to praying daily, following the Big Book method of recovery, and wanting to start her own ministry for at-risk youth would be a great train to catch for introducing my name in the social justice community, I thought. Even with such skewed intentions, I was able to just sit and listen. She beamed with excitement after court hearings, the completion of appointed rehab programs, or the chance meeting of one of her former cell-mates now also trying to transform her skill set to what Jeneth called "hustling for Jesus."

Things were still optimistic well into the springtime. But it didn't take longer than early summer to be reminded of the limitations of fair weather, and of noble intentions. The spiral downward started when Jeneth got sideswiped on her bicycle on the way home from turning in a bag of aluminum at the recycling plant. The truck kept pummeling down the road, meanwhile Jeneth lie with what would, in examination, prove to be three broken ribs and an unaligned hip. This forced her to retire from the side jobs she held throughout the week for cash once Food Stamps and Social Security benefits ran out.

I called her out of the blue the Friday of Memorial Day weekend. Her speech slurred as she wiped the sleep out of her eyes. "I've been suicidal, Audrey," she said squarely. She'd missed her last two mental health appointments and didn't have the $3 cash needed to refill her prescriptions. Her forty-fourth birthday was coming up that Tuesday, but both her mom and sister had once again backed out of her life. She needed groceries, toilet paper, and tampons. When I picked her up one of the last times before she got evicted, she began crying softly. "What about calling Kim for someone to hang out with, or that friend of yours you lived with while on home detention?" I proposed. She simply shook her head. "Everyone's too busy with their own lives," she said.

I was struck, at that moment, by how singularly important it is, for each of us, just to have someone to talk to. Aside from all of the social programs and human service agencies—the cadre of which I was still trying to familiarize myself with in my new position—aside from the prescriptions, AA witnesses, rent-assistance, and food stamps. Jeneth's primary need was someone she could splurge with on a "Big Gulp" from time to time. To kick back and laugh with, even if, after the last bout, she was uncertain what life had in store.

*Ask not how you can be of service, but how you can enter into friendship.*

> Our commitment ... consists ... in an attentiveness which considers the other "in a certain sense as one with ourselves." ... We are called to find Christ in them, to lend our voice to their causes, but also to be their friends, to listen to them, to speak for them and to embrace the mysterious wisdom which God wishes to share with us through them. (*Evangelii Gaudium*, 198)

To put it shortly, if we were all high schoolers, and had some virtuous strain of the tendency to choose our friends based off of what they can do for us, we would all want to be hanging out with the poor. What could be of greater value, after all, than the realization of your dependence on the mercy of God? This is something I try to introduce in conversation with parishes and agencies every time I see a soup kitchen where the clients and the volunteers only make contact through the plexi-glass window. Or, a Saint Vincent de Paul Society "Adopt a Family" program that that never allows the two families to meet out of concerns of privacy. Francis is challenging us to strive beyond the limitations of our traditional understanding of "serving" the poor—it is a one-sided exchange in which the categories of who is giving and receiving are too fixed. He is requiring us to mature in our faith—to bridge past the need for black and white environments where the most difficult part of how we communicate the Gospel has to do with volume and diction, and start familiarizing ourselves with relating to people, fostering the virtues of understanding and gratitude.

This is one area in which the Church will be called to do some major lifting during Francis' pontificate. The most severe poverty that can befall a man or woman is he or she living as though they are excluded from Christ's salvation on account of the merit or content of their life. One basic way we can start befriending the poor is to return to a simple, authentic language and example to introduce them to how Christ is present in their lives.

Monday, I enter into the county jail. I volunteer to bring the book cart into the female blocks for a few hours in the afternoon. I'm always surprised by how much the sterile, cold environment still affects me. Each time I leave, the rest of the afternoon is spent in deep reflection, running over the names and stark faces of the women, the blare of the TV in the room, the crispness of the awkwardness of relating to the stories the women freely share. "No, my daughter and I ain't talkin' these days," said one white, frail woman with crooked glasses. "That's why I got thrown in here again—her truancy. I didn't know my boyfriend had started touching her again when he came back around last month. He gave me this," she says as she pulls up her bangs to reveal the fresh scar.

The idea is that, since friends like to spend time around each other, the more we open ourselves up to horizontal relationships with the poor, the more we will be able to participate in life together in ways that are mutually beneficial. No longer is it just service projects and donations, but where we go grocery shopping, how we spend our weekends, to which playground we take our kids. Justice begins to be approachable when seen closer to what it actually is: a daily, participatory, contact sport. With the Holy Spirit's assistance, we will become able to see "the poor" in every situation. We will begin molding our civic institutions and social systems, our parks and parades, our museums and libraries with the weak and frail in mind, asking ourselves how we can make them as accessible and inclusive as possible.

Pope Francis is not the first pope to emphasize the Church's preference for the poor. He's just the first, in our lived experience, to embody it so vividly. He invites us to do the same.

It will be by going out, sharing, asking, looking into one another's eyes, getting to know one another, and looking forward to a future when the Gospel will reach the ends of the earth. Our Pope has broken open the Church's imagination to see love for the poor, not as some kind of guilty obligation, added layer of responsibility, romanticized ideal, or purely intellectual exercise, but as a way of life.

Audrey Anweiler terminated studies in Social Communications at a Pontifical University in Rome, Italy, months before Pope Benedict XVI's resignation, to join the Catholic Worker community in Louisville, Kentucky. Today she is grateful to be working as a Coordinator for Social Justice Ministries in the Diocese of Fort Wayne–South Bend, Indiana.

# Contemplating the Whole Horse: Allen Tate and the Catholic Sensibility

Louis D. Rubin, Jr. acknowledged in the 1976 reintroduction to *I'll Take My Stand* (1930) that Allen Tate and his Vanderbilt friends were not trying to reassert a neo-Confederate nostalgia upon their readers. Admittedly, the book's title does not help one get over the association with the Civil War, but in truth these men of letters were addressing problems associated with industrialization and what Rubin identifies as the "worship of material progress as an end in itself."

Contemporary biographers of George Washington and Thomas Jefferson know that before you talk about dead Southern white men you have to offer some sort of explanation that borders on an apology. People who have no sense of history become ill at ease with figures that wrote rules of conduct for themselves or worse, owned slaves. So, the first task of this essay is to put readers at ease. In Thomas A. Underwood's biography *Allen Tate: Orphan of the South* he describes his subject as someone shaped by his Southern upbringing, but who later distanced himself from his inherited racism. Tate differs little from, say, Walker Percy, another Southern writer who reconciled matters of race with his newfound Catholic faith, but at the same time did not reject what was most precious to him in regard to elements of Southern culture.

If there is any guilt by association it lies with Southern culture's connection with Europe. More specifically, it lies in its connection with medieval Europe and a Catholic sensibility. The Middle Ages have managed to retain an even longer history of derision in comparison to the Antebellum South. The advent of the Enlightenment put a dunce hat on the Church and made her sit in the corner while science was escorted to the front of the class. Watching from their designated spot in the room, the Faithful have seen the fruits of the Enlightenment and the culture of death it has produced. The Vanderbilt Twelve were taking advantage of a moment in history to point out that the Enlightenment, and its industrial manifestation, was a Faustian bargain.

We are now left to pick up the pieces. Tate's meditation on the Catholic sensibility is a good place to start if the Faithful—the radically Catholic—want to rebuild something more suitable for human flourishing. This essay looks for love among the ruins. Fortunately, the construction has already begun.

✳ ✳ ✳

A year before the publication of *I'll Take My Stand* the Stock Market collapsed, sending shock waves to the four corners of the earth. Most American intellectuals sensed a political, economic, and social realignment could be expected, but what shape it would take was uncertain. Centralized planning by the government to stabilize the economy seemed the preferred solution, especially when considering the threat of a socialist revolution. The country had already gotten use to "big" ways of doing its business. The ubiquitous presence of corporate advertising and marketing techniques had been reshaping the American landscape for at least fifty years.

The authors of *I'll Take My Stand* believed big solutions were what got the country into an economic crisis in the first place. Decentralization of economic and political power, therefore, was the best restorative solution, and the South understood this better than the North because its memory of small things still lingered. The Nashville Twelve were not economists, but humanists. They were poets. Tate was well aware that the artist could offer up a prophetic voice, that all the great molders of Western civilization had been painters, writers, and mystics.

Tate's essay, "Remarks on the Southern Religion," contemplated the Whole Horse. The metaphor stood for what he thought was true religion, and thus reality itself, visible an invisible. The problem with modern man was that he could no longer perceive the Whole Horse; he could only see one half of it, or perhaps the other half, but not a unified object cropping blue grass on the lawn. Tate's thesis attempted to locate a sensibility that existed in medieval Europe. "The South could be ignorant of Europe," Tate says, "because it *was* Europe."

Tate maintained moderns saw only the utilitarian value of the horse, what he called "infallible workability." Half-horse religionists believed in horsepower, assembly lines, and smokestacks. They could not see the beauty and grace of the horse which comprised the other half, and which formed a separate category that had little to do with the first one. Tate believed half-horse religionists took a Long View of history—the progressive view—where B is always an improvement over A that came before it. The half-horse religionist was incapable of pointing to a more ideal way of life from the past. Therefore, the Middle Ages would always remain anathema.

According to Tate, the Cartesian mind-split originated with the Reformation's drive for individual spiritual autonomy and the Enlightenment's drive for secular self-determination. Both Protestantism and Scientism maintained a Long View of history and a controlling materialism. (If anyone doubts this, consider for a moment the character of the Second Great Awakening with its manipulating altar calls and techniques of inducing revival.) At the heart of Tate's essay is the claim that the Protestant South failed to give an adequate defense of its society because it was, after all, the heir of a "non-agrarian and trading religion; hardly a religion at all, but a result of secular ambition."

This is a harsh criticism of Protestantism, but Tate's point is that had the South possessed a unified religion—a Whole Horse religion— it might have insulated itself from the ravishing effects of industrialism. Tate says, "the social structure of the South began to break down two generations after the Civil War," and that its collapse was predictable because "the social structure depends on the economic structure, and economic conviction is the secular image of religion."

In short, Tate is declaring that had the South been predominantly Catholic it might have preserved its agrarian way of life; it might have become the exemplar of Jeffersonian democracy ideally perceived. *Ideally* perceived, that is. For even Jefferson himself did not understand the connection of between a society's religion and its economy. Tate uses Jefferson as a symbolic figure to demonstrate how the seeds of the Enlightenment were already present at the nation's founding. As John Glass points out in a forthcoming book on Tate, the country's third president was a person who embodied the South's virtues as well as its flaws. His actions were paradoxical. Here is a man who penned the Declaration of Independence, and then kept his slaves; a man who sunk his justification of liberty in Nature's God, and then cut the supernatural events out of the Bible.

Tate believed that inherent in Protestantism was a defective gene, the mind-dividing element of the Enlightenment, the same DNA that produced modern capitalism's worship of material progress. One has to look no further than Max Weber to find most of this spelled out. While Weber misrepresented some of Calvin's teaching and did not adequately link the Enlightenment to his thesis, he was generally on the mark by asserting that market capitalism would not have taken off were it not for Protestants granting it permission. The early Reformers did not preach wealth accumulation from their pulpits because they were essentially medievalists themselves, but second and third generation Calvinists adopted the tenets of capitalism with its emphasis on specialization, division of labor, and the shift of production away from the home to the factory. The new American republic would favor the Protestant middle class, maximize individual freedom, and be religiously tolerant. Unfortunately, the Constitution said nothing about the family, nor did it address spiritual or aesthetic values.

To fully understand Tate's mediation a word should be said about these missing spiritual and aesthetic values, which had been around for at least a thousand years in the West. Many twentieth century Catholic writers from J. R. R. Tolkien to Thomas Merton to Tate were pulled toward a medieval vision because it represented an age when economics, politics, and the social ordering existed in a kind of harmony under the banner of Christianity. More importantly, the natural and the supernatural existed in harmony; the one had not been teased out from the other. The Catholic imagination is sacramental: the Creation is sacred, human beings are sacred, and the ordinary is sacred. The medieval vision does not diminish the notion of sin; rather, it accentuates it, for all evil is a perversion of the good. God stepped into the world— became mud like us—in order to purchase the good world back from the Fall. The incarnation of Christ is central to the Catholic imagination. The physical world, as perceived through the senses, teaches us about God's created order. What we see, hear, touch, smell, and taste— if one pays close attention and is honest in his thinking—will declare what is right, true, and good. Those who have been very perceptive and very honest, like Aristotle, are not enemies of the faith, but some of its best contributors.

Catholic writers like Flannery O'Connor grounded their fiction in the muck and mire of human relationships for the purpose of describing a much wider band of reality. In this way, the visible declares the invisible; the tangible proclaims the sublime. O'Connor says in her essay "The Church and the Fiction Writer" that, "When fiction is made according to its nature, it should reinforce our sense of the supernatural by grounding it in concrete, observable reality. If the writer uses his eyes in the real security of the Faith, he will be obliged to use them honestly, and his sense of mystery, and acceptance of it, will be increased." Likewise, Tolkien's fantasy world of Middle Earth is actually our world, only seen through a medieval sensibility, one that does not divorce the natural from the supernatural.

Without the ability to *remember* this Catholic sensibility we are impotent. Contemplating the Whole Horse empowers us to act. And act (or react) we must do as Tate insists: "Reaction is the most radical of programs; it aims at cutting away the overgrowth and getting back to the roots." Tate says the reaction will be *violent,* not that he is making some sort of call to arms, but because for moderns to return to premodern sensibilities it requires a radical act of the will. Tate closes his essay by reasserting the heart of his proposition: "As we have said, economy is the secular image of religious conviction." In other words, there is a connection between a culture's religion and its economic ordering.

\* \* \*

Cutting away centuries of Enlightenment overgrowth seems like a daunting task. But one has to begin somewhere, and the jungle is not going to cut itself down, at least not until Jesus comes back. From a practical standpoint, as Americans we are confined to the limitations of our Constitution to create anew. So unless someone wants to start a new country, we have to work in the world in which we find ourselves. All efforts will be humble ones, however large or small. In considering a hardy Christian culture, a seamless anti-Cartesian philosophy, and a humane economy, there are already a number of building projects to be found that are serving to hold out the Whole Horse.

First among these projects is Christian education on two important fronts — homeschooling and classical education. There is nothing more Whole Horse than for parents to opt out of the system and bring their children back into the household, not only to educate them, but also for them to participate in the domesticity of the home. Homeschooling is medieval, and rightly so.

Classical Christian education employs the medieval trivium (grammar, dialectic, and rhetoric) to good effect. Interestingly, the surge of classical schools is primarily a movement within conservative Reformed Protestant circles. When speaking to classical Christian school administrators one soon discovers they understand the negative aspects of the Cartesian mind-split. A typical reading list for a high school student might include Luther and Calvin, but students are just as likely to read Aristotle, Augustine, and Aquinas. The growth of homeschooling and classical Christian education within the United States is serving to restore a holistic Christian sensibility.

Another encouraging development is the formation of confessional Protestants who seek a Catholic sensibility in matters of faith and culture. In his *First Things* declaration Peter Leithart says a Reformational Catholic is someone who "cheerfully acknowledges that he shares creeds with Roman Catholics" and "welcomes reforms and reformulations as hopeful signs that we might at last stake out common ground beyond the barricades." His vision incorporates a piety that is communal and sacramental as well as worship that follows historical liturgical patterns. The growth of classical Christian education and the advent of Reformational Catholics have the potential to bring Rome and Geneva in closer proximity in the twenty-first century.

Not only do we need Catholic-minded Protestants, we also need Catholic-minded Catholics.

Joseph Pearce is one such person. Turning out a book almost every year since 1996, Pearce has resurrected the Whole Horse by writing biographies of G. K. Chesterton, Hilaire Belloc, J. R. R. Tolkien, Oscar Wilde, and Alexander Solzhenitsyn. He has tied Shakespeare to the Catholic Church, explored Catholic poetry, and reasserted E. F. Schumacher's proposal that small is beautiful in matters of economics. Pearce, who has assumed the directorship of the Center for Faith & Culture at Aquinas College in Nashville, has committed himself to evangelizing the imagination through literature, art, and cultural engagement.

Finally, those who wish to hold out the Whole Horse need to continue working on their *shtick*—creative ways to get their message across to increasingly dissatisfied customers feed up with a perpetual life of consumption yet unable to articulate what is wrong with the world. By way of example, Schumacher gave us some useful phraseology to promote economies of scale. In addition to his claim that "small is beautiful" he spoke of "technologies with a human face" and being "homecomers." Distributism is an accurate word, historically speaking, for the type of economic ordering Whole Horse proponents seek, but it will stifle a conversation the instant it is uttered. Microcapitalism is a preferable term, as well as Alexander Solzhenitsyn's "democracy of small places." We might also try these on for size: sacramental societies, deliberate communities, and new parish life.

The creation of such communities can only follow a fired imagination. The will to act on the vision will incur the violence of the salmon swimming upstream. But upstream we must go, to spawn something better for our children.

 Arthur W. Hunt III is author of
*Surviving Technopolis: Finding Balance
in Our New Man-Made Environments*
(Pickwick, 2013).

# Cucumbers and the Future of the Neighborhood

Last summer I decided to try a little something new in the garden: cucumbers in containers. So I started a bunch of seeds to transplant. As I was leaning over to place the seeds in their little trays, I lost my balance and dropped the seeds onto the tray haphazardly. It was unremarkable really, and if I'd had more time, I might have re-placed the seeds, but didn't.

A week or so later, they all emerged. Of the dozen or so cells, there was at least one seedling in each cell, but several had something like eight. Some had five or six. One had ten. I noted that I would have to get around to thinning them, planted them in my containers, and moved on, pausing to note that the two singletons were remarkably large and robust: no thinning required, perfect for planting out in a manicured cucumber plot.

Six weeks later, I realized I'd maybe, kinda forgotten about my container cucumber project, possibly watering it only four times. I rushed out to see what had happened. The singletons were flat out dead; the pairs were struggling to survive; but the group of ten ... actually looked pretty good. It seemed that the more were in the grouping, the better the grouping had fared.

I initially took this as divine revelation about family size. As the year has come full circle, though, and I keep returning to the ripe metaphor this presents, I keep learning from it. Now, the first thing is obvious. Keep your workspace clear of shoes so you don't spill seeds. But that aside, I think I may have been offered a small bit of wisdom about faith and community.

About four years ago, looking for a home for our family of six, my husband and I decided that home prices in the fair city of Ann Arbor, Michigan, were never going to be rational, or even just reasonable, so we decided to look to a darker city: Saginaw, Michigan, ninety miles to the north. My parents had relocated to Saginaw in the late '90s and it seemed like a good idea to be close to family. And the home prices were great.

We had this idea about saving the world with the way we lived our lives. It was simple really. Moving from the Detroit suburbs to an impoverished Michigan city was the kind of change that we had been advocating for some time; and not only would we do this, we would encourage others to join us. It would weave everything together and our lives lived would be a direct action. We were blissfully unaware of our status as robust singleton seedlings en route to a barely watered container.

Now you have to understand that a neighborhood—an old city neighborhood—is really a living, breathing organism, not unlike seeds in soil. Children are born and raised there, their parents grow old there, and when the organism is healthy, some of the children stay and raise families of their own. People look at that healthy neighborhood, and they think to themselves that one day they'll move to that lovely neighborhood with trees that touch in the middle of the street, where neighbors chat casually on a Saturday afternoon, and where children ride bikes to the corner store for bubble gum and sodas. And the lifecycle continues.

But sometimes, the organism gets an infection. It might get infected with a racial divide, or socioeconomic divides. Other times, outside forces might start starving a neighborhood economically, removing jobs and resources that the community had come to rely on. Whatever it is, something catches hold and the children keep growing up and leaving. And slowly, painfully, the thing that makes the neighborhood what it was just withers away.

Sometimes neighborhoods remake and rebuild themselves with transplants, and that rebirth and resurgence can be remarkable. But still other times, a neighborhood will slide into a terrible chronic illness: absentee landlords. Now I'm not talking about the guy or the gal that rents out a granny-flat apartment. I'm talking about the landlords on the other side of the state, out-of-state even, that are just pumping out money and taking a tax deduction. That's a dangerous neighborhood illness. Our adopted neighborhood is fighting to stay on top of its absentee landlordism, in addition to a nearly complete lack of jobs, and a lingering racism hiccup. This is quite the scene, and it seems so quaint now to think about how awesome (!) our "direct-action of living" was going to be while we're just trying to keep the yard mowed, the weeds pulled, the prayers prayed, the children fed, the baby nursed, the crayon off the walls, the Mass attended, the lessons learned, and the job worked.

So, first things first: we started having meetings. We pulled together some good folks and started doing some things. The one really great thing that came from those efforts and that is still going strong is our farm market co-op. Several folks chipped in bit of cash, and Saginaw Harvest is a cooperative of urban micro-farms in Saginaw County. We sell a wide variety of organic produce and eggs at the Downtown Saginaw Farmer's Market. But alas, our neighborhood is ill, folks keep moving, and we keep losing some of our mojo.

Next up, we connected to a great Catholic home-school coop, and got our children plugged in. Those connections have led to another cooperative, a "mother's club." We get together each week and clean each other's homes. The children play and the mommies chat. It is a heaven sent support network, but the moms are scattered across three counties. It's a Catholic home-school group, but there just aren't enough Catholic home-schoolers in the neighborhood to make a go of something like this.

The other life curves we've navigated since our move have been death in our extended family, two births, and a job loss. My father had passed away before we moved up, so we were especially motivated to move close by to make sure our children had as much time with my mother as they were able. Also, my eldest brother had been caring for both my parents in their later years, and we wanted to share that work with him. We had two and a half wonderful years here with my mother, and a Thanksgiving with many family members together before she passed. That was a gift without equal. But now in the aftermath, my brother struggles to find work in the area and to care for my parents' large city parcel—2.5 acres—along with three buildings that all need maintenance. He wonders if there is any way in this job market he can stay here in Saginaw and make enough money to maintain the family land and houses. Frankly, after an abrupt lay-off last March, and six months without work, we're wondering if we can even keep our little raft afloat. It's harder than you might expect in 2014 to find a telecommuting job for a tech worker.

Our neighborhood association meets monthly (the last Wednesday of the month at the Lutheran seminary) and is, frankly, the last line of defense against what ails this place. The good men and women of the neighborhood meet up and talk about any crime problems, invite speakers, get the word out about various city initiatives, plan garden walks and parties, select block captains, and welcome transplants to the neighborhood.

As is often the case, it is the births that give me hope. We've had such wonderful outpourings of support when our two Saginaw babies were born. People still know how to do that, especially in an old city neighborhood. The ladies keep tab on the new babies, and show up—unannounced—with dinner, love, and goodies, for months after the baby comes home. It is perfect. The only concern I'm left with, is who will replace these precious women when the time comes? Who's going to take over nurturing this neighborhood's immune system? Will they be the one or two children struggling to maintain the family's inherited wealth? Or will there be enough social capital to support the coming generation in keeping this organism alive and healthy?

As I wondered somewhat fearfully about the answers to these questions, I came across a piece by Will Seath in *Fare Forward*, called "This Is What We Do." In it he chronicles the Catholic revival of a little slice of Hyattsville, Maryland, around a Catholic parish and school by—get this—transplants! And suddenly, I'm reminded that we're transplants to Saginaw, and that we'd initially hoped to encourage more transplants to join us here. This is when the metaphor really hits me about my cucumbers: We had never intended to be robust singletons in a carefully tended monocrop.

From the very outset we had hoped to have and be a part of something very much like the intentional Catholic community in Hyattsville. We had hoped that we could be the first folks that made moving to a place with a decidedly uncertain future a little less scary for other folks. We had looked forward to plunging deep into our parish—just a short walk away—and finding a cohort for our children. But that cohort has already moved out of the neighborhood.

So what's holding us back from a renaissance like Hyattsville's? It's very simple: there are no jobs to speak of here, and there's no mass transit to get to where the jobs are. What few jobs there are in public service and hospitals are held by folks in this neighborhood, most of whom are nearing retirement age, or by folks that live as far away from the city as they possibly can. But this *driving into the city for your job while living and paying taxes elsewhere* situation is completely unsustainable. It's the long term fear I have about our Mother's Cooperative: we can't tool around three counties in private automobiles for the next 20 years. We may not be able to do it for the next five years. And it's the long term fear about staying here, having to drive across three counties to get to work, that is just not a realistic or moral long-term strategy in a world of scarce resources.

So what to do? We need to get more transplants into the soil here, and we can't support anymore transplants without jobs. What if the transplants brought their jobs with them? What if the transplants we encouraged were folks with an entrepreneurial spirit, and looking for an opportunity? That could be amazing, and I've written about that before. The start-ups that make it would certainly be the next anchors of the community going forward. Yet that seems like half an answer to me now. Many start-ups fail, and things are precarious enough as it is.

But another opportunity has presented itself, and it echoes Hyattsville's story. Our parish's school closed this spring. There just are not enough students to keep the school open, so the diocese has consolidated Saginaw's two remaining K–8 schools. How could a parish re-imagine the school space to bring in families, and replace the holes left by so many families that have fled the city? I'm not sure of the answer to this question. But I think it's the seed that we need to germinate here.

Maybe this is a revelation about family size, but perhaps not nuclear families. I think this is an insight about the size of your spiritual family and communal family. Neither of these sorts of families can weather adversity alone. And if these are not adverse times, then there is no such thing as adversity.

 Grace Potts is a Roman Catholic wife and mother of six children. Politically, she's so conservative that she's progressive; or is it so progressive that she's conservative? No matter—you probably get the idea. She likes hiking and camping, quilting, cooking, antiques, and contra dancing.

# Steamed Pork Buns and the Altar of Relevance

It's a personal truth I've found that the small and trivial things, the things that seem insignificant, are often the ones which will come to leave the deepest mark on you, the ones which shade your convictions and your frame of mind the most, in the end. G. K. Chesterton once remarked, in *What's Wrong with the World*, that "with the red hair of one she-urchin in the gutter I will set fire to all of modern civilisation." For me, all of radicalism, of conservatism, of Orthodoxy, of *sobornyi* and the glorification of the saints, could very well have been inspired by the most humble and ubiquitous of Chinese snack-foods: a simple steamed pork bun. Well, actually, in my case it was more like two *long* (bamboo steamers) of the things, with ten of the two-bite sweet-and-savoury-and-satisfying *baozi* each, costing five *kuai* each (then about eighty cents), which comprised my lunch on a regular basis on my second visit to China.

The *baozi* itself is a venerable dish hailing from the rural, tradition-ally-poor and traditionally-rebellious Chinese West—Sichuan, to be exact. Tradition has it that they were invented by the scholar and mili-tary tactician Zhuge Liang during the Three Kingdoms period, about two hundred years after the birth of Christ, as a convenient and hy-gienic food meant to be offered as sacrifice, and to stem a plague that had broken out amongst the Sichuanese military. But they have since been adopted by the entire country, and each region has its own particular variant of the pork bun.

China is, after all, a nation of gourmands. One of those things that will strike you about China on first impression is that the familial and entrepreneurial spirits of its people meld with the cultural penchant for seeking out the best foods to create a practically distributist-looking patchwork of such family-owned *getihu* restaurants on every other urban back road, specialising in everything from spicy breakfast soups to cumin roasted lamb kebabs and beer. Sadly, high and usurious barriers of access to credit, combined with a continuing enclosures policy under "reform and opening" leading to high urban migration from poor rural provinces like Anhui and Henan, practically guarantee a high turnover rate. But the particular restaurant which served these delectable things was a little mom-and-pop shop in Beijing, run by a couple from Hangzhou. Memory plays funny tricks. I can no longer remember the *baoziguan* owner's face, but I can remember the fellow's half-smile, his weathered hands and his voice as he asked me: *"Baozi—liang long?"* "Two steamers of pork buns?"—whenever he saw me appear around the corner.

It was quite the popular joint. I was introduced to it by one of the other exchange students at Capital Normal, with whom I generally got along quite well. Being so close to the campus, it was a frequent stop for students and tourists of all stripes, as well as for the Beijingers who lived on that stretch of West Third Ring Road. The most common of the foreigners were Americans and Brits, but you could find Israelis, Iraqis, Koreans, Russians there as well—at one point, the place was packed with an entire guided-tour's worth of Japanese day-trippers.

I was there in 2006. The whole city was just beginning to prepare, at that time, for the 2008 Summer Olympics. The big countdown clock had been erected on Tian'anmen (500+ days ahead of time, so it counted!), and all the big new contracted construction projects were underway everywhere. It was, as mentioned earlier, the second time I'd been to China—and already the car-to-bicycle ratio there had ballooned since I'd been there just one year previous. New construction projects were happening on every corner, including on the block where the *baoziguan* was. High-rises, hotels, office parks—all slabs of concrete, steel and tinted glass. And more often than not, what they replaced were the scallop-tile roofed houses of some old *hutong* which had been there for many decades, if not many centuries.

The entire face of the city changed even in the nine months I was there. It is (or was then) another truism of first encounters with China that the visitor will be struck and disoriented by the juxtaposition of the glitteringly modern with the breathtakingly ancient. Neighbourhoods dating back to the Yuan dynasty decked out in neon. Qing-era parks and temples surrounded on all sides by traffic and skyscrapers. The infamous Starbucks in the Forbidden City (which closed shortly after I left Beijing). But it appeared to me that too much development, too many projects, were moving the city entirely in one direction — at the expense, so it appeared to me then, of its soul.

"Too many good things have gotten sacrificed upon the altar of relevance."

My father is not one for giving voice to conservative views. He is as devout a liberal Protestant as one is likely to find, taking theological inspiration particularly from Alfred Whitehead and John Cobb, Jr. But in our many discussions and disputes over the broader matters this is one thing that he has told me that has always sort of stuck with me, and has never really gone away. Each time I saw a crane towering over an old *hutong*, that saying of my father's came back with more force.

True enough: I was the outsider, who had no true experience of the place other than that of the outsider, the foreigner. Who was I to make the call of how or where China should modernise and develop? To tell the truth, I was nobody. But all the same, I watched and noted. There was a powerful sense of loss — the sacrifice that the people of Beijing were making unasked of the life of their old neighbourhoods. That *baoziguan* I'd frequented on a thrice-weekly basis is long gone now. I went back to Beijing two months ago for the purposes of getting my daughter's nationality papers in order, and decided to revisit for memory's sake my old stomping-grounds. To my dismay, the entire block was unrecognisable to me, practically right until I got up to the gates of the Capital Normal international campus (itself a modernist ziggurat of burnished steel and glass).

By then, of course, China had changed me. The levelling of the small and beautiful and well-loved, to make way for the imposing-yet-purely-utilitarian had bewildered and confused me at the time, but now the injustice of it also saddens and angers me. There is intrinsic value in being small, and intrinsic value in being beautiful, and intrinsic value in being old and loved (though that is all value that often goes unseen and unmarked in the cost-benefit analysis). The study of Chinese society on a personal level, in Buddhist temples and in Christian churches, as well as the intellectual and sociological canon which undergirded it, led me to an appreciation of what rootedness there had been in my own life, and to a search for the missing links of my family history. And, odd though it may sound coming from a young Westerner to say that the philosophy of Confucius led me to a deeper appreciation of the traditions of the Church—in both its Latin and its Greek manifestations, but ultimately to find my way home to the Greek—it holds true in my case at least.

China justly boasts a five thousand year-old civilisation, and the forms of the Good it has produced and kept down the ages are many, but many of those forms are under threat. It is not that I fret for the loss of pork buns or anything of the kind; these are likely to be around for another eighteen hundred years at least! But I do indeed worry for the civilisation's intellectual, civic and moral traditions. These have been battered—but God willing not yet crushed!—by over a century and a half of exploitation by Western powers, revolutionary republicanism, militant communism and now a crassly mercenary consumer capitalism. Each in turn has sought to overturn these traditions and to sacrifice them to the spirit of the times upon the altar of relevance. And I worry for the people who have been and are being displaced by a market which seeks to uproot them and to wring them of all their value before discarding them, and a government whose care for these people seems limited at best. I worry that it may sound melodramatic or alarmist, but I still must ask: what and how much of this civilisation will be left once our children come of age, and their children after them?

To be catholic, in the sense in which it is meant in the creed—that is to say, from καθόλου, which can mean "according to the unity of all" or "according to the whole" scope of reality—simply barricading ourselves behind the civilizational wall of "the West" is not an option. One of the most beautiful things about the Orthodox faith is that it has, without ever compromising the transcendental dogmas and truths at its core, embedded in the life of each individual Church the little-"t" traditions and folkways not just of Greeks and Palestinians but also of Slavs, Armenians, Central Asians, Egyptians and Ethiopians. The Good is where you find it; from standing firm upon one set of transcendent values, a holy, apostolic and catholic Christianity is indeed better able, in all its various forms and places, to embrace and transform it.

Matthew Cooper is a convert to Eastern Orthodoxy and parishioner of the Moscow Patriarchate; a happy husband to his wife Jessie and father to his daughter Eleanore; a graduate of Kalamazoo College in philosophy and of the University of Pittsburgh–GSPIA in development economics; and an English teacher in Baotou, China. He is heavily influenced in his religious convictions by the Russian religious philosophers Nicolas Berdyaev, Alexis Khomiakoff and John Kireevsky, though in deference to C. S. Lewis he bashfully asserts that he will in short order get to work on reading older and Greeker authors. He seems to have settled on 'monarcho-syndicalist' as an appropriate summation of his political commitments.

# A Relationship with Creation

## The Synthesis of the World

With a 6'3" surfboard under my arm and the picture of an Indian guru in my pocket, I took off for an eleven-month trip around the world. I was a young, raggedy backpacker insatiably searching for adventure within the wonders of nature; looking for happiness in the lost islands of Indonesia and forgotten monasteries of Bhutan.

The surfboard and the guru express a thousand words about what was going on inside my 18-year-old, borderline millennial, head and heart. I was holding on to my past and looking to the future; groping for God with no education about divinity; searching for simplicity having lived a life of privilege; trying to be unique but expected to conform like everyone else; wanting to be selfless while being hedonistically self-centered; getting lost but hoping to be found; searching for meaning in an empty world. These non-linear ideas and emotionally disjointed longings were sincere, authentic, and while unique, so "Generation Y."

What did not follow the generational trends however was where my search ended: I found Jesus, became Catholic and am now a consecrated religious brother. How on earth did the Church find me? The answer is simple in theory, difficult in practice. All I needed was to meet people who pointed me to Jesus. He did the rest. I met a group of

Christians who helped me understand that my quest was for Christ; in that light I was able to reinterpret and redeem my search.

All this is best expressed in this key passage of the Puebla document from the Latin American Conference of Bishops (CELAM), so beloved and so often quoted by Cardinal Bergoglio:[1]

> If the Church does not reinterpret the religion of… the people, a void will be produced that will be filled by sects, secularized political messianisms, a consumerism that produces tedium and indifference or pagan pansexualism. Once again the Church faces the problem: what it does not assume in Christ is not redeemed and becomes a new idol with the malice of old.[2]

Infused with the spirit of Vatican II, this passage rests on the premise that human beings are religious by nature and always searching for God. The Church must assume human longings and experiences, however naïve or misguided they may be, and redeem them in Christ.[3] It is

---

[1] *El Verdadero Poder es el Servicio*

[2] http://www.celam.org/doc_conferencias/Documento_Conclusivo_Puebla. pdf, 469. For World Youth Day in Brazil, Pope Francis said pretty much the same thing but in simpler language. He compared the flight of Christians from the Church to the disciples of Emmaus: "We need a Church unafraid of going forth into their night… of entering into their conversation. We need a Church able to dialogue with those disciples who… are wandering aimlessly, alone, with their own disappointment, disillusioned by a Christianity now considered barren, fruitless soil, incapable of generating meaning… [We need] persons able to step into the night without being overcome by the darkness and losing their bearings; able to listen to people's dreams without being seduced and to share their disappointments without losing hope and becoming bitter; able to sympathize with the brokenness of others without losing their own strength and identity."

[3] "We must be bold enough to discover new signs and new symbols, new flesh to embody and communicate the word… including those unconventional modes of beauty which may mean little to the evangelizers, yet prove particularly attractive for others." In short, the Church must engage people where they are at just like Jesus did—the promiscuous woman at the well, Zacheus on the roadside, the disciples of Emmaus in their desolation.

the same thing that Francis means when he says in *Evangelii Gaudium,* "Where your synthesis is, there your heart will be also."4 The "synthesis" is how people make sense of the world; what they have put together amidst the contradictions of life.5 Faith must reach the real person, their synthesis, from the converted inner synthesis of the apostle. This is the difficult part: only a true, converted heart (synthesis) can point others to Jesus. A faith that is preached, received and practiced as scattered formulas, ideals and customs is not a real faith and does not last.

## Pope Francis and the Environment

In my search for the wise guru and the perfect wave I met Christians who were able to evangelize my synthesis: meaning, adventure, nature, pleasure, solitude, friendship, freedom, depth, transcendence, truth and god. All these eventually made sense and found their place in the light of God. When Francis urges us to "go out into the streets" to speak of mercy, when he asks "who am I to judge?" or "these days we do not have a very good relationship with creation, do we?"6 he is telling the Church to embrace the world's concerns and interpret its longings in the light of Christ. He is situating himself in the people's worldview, speaking to his flock in their own language. He is evangelizing the synthesis.

In one of his last magisterial catecheses, entitled "How to Speak about God in Our Times?", Pope Benedict was describing the world's synthesis. The Church has always relied on the "signs of the times"7 to

---

4 *El Verdadero Poder es el Servicio;* EG 143. This speech and main ideas were pretty much copied and pasted into *Evangelii Gaudium.*

5 In Bergoglio's words, "The vital synthesis, this which is indefinable in words, since it would require them all, this symbolic and living nucleus … is the theological place where the preacher must vitally situate himself. That is to say, the challenge of an inculturated preaching is in evangelizing the synthesis, not scattered ideas or values."

6 http://w2.vatican.va/content/francesco/en/speeches/2013/march/documents/papa-francesco_20130316_rappresentanti-media.html

7 On his deathbed, Saint John XXIII said that "the moment has come to discern the signs of the times, to seize the opportunity and to look far ahead."

discern the question of how to approach the world, and the Pope Emeritus spelled out these signs clearly and explicitly: "the wish for authenticity, the yearning for transcendence, and concern to safeguard Creation and to communicate fearlessly the response that faith in God offers."[8] Authenticity, transcendence, and care for creation. Here lies, in broad strokes, the synthesis of the modern world. And care for creation stands out in being a specific concern rather than a human longing. Pope Francis embodies all of these signs in his very person, and is decidedly engaging the concern for creation.

It is now rumored that Pope Francis' first encyclical will also be the Church's first ever encyclical dedicated to ecology. On May 7th, 2014, the UN climate chief spoke to over one thousand people at St. Paul's Cathedral in London and said that she is "trying to figure out how to use the opportunity" of the Pope's encyclical, since "everyone's expecting it."[9] After years of tracking Papal statements on ecology, which usually were a curious afterthought for most people, especially the world's political leaders, it is hard to believe the change of tide. Now the Pope sets the agenda, and the UN piggybacks on the momentum!

There is a lot of speculation about what the Pope will say in the encyclical. Of course the hint given by Fr. Lombardi on "human ecology" suggests many things already, as do the different Papal statements and messages uttered to this day.[10] But the most important clue to the es-

---

The Vatican Council which he convoked stated that, "to carry out such a task [evangelization], the Church has always had the duty of scrutinizing the signs of the times and of interpreting them in the light of the Gospel." Pope Francis declined to offer "a detailed and complete analysis of contemporary reality" in *Evangelii Gaudium* but said that an "ever watchful scrutiny of the signs of the times" is "a grave responsibility" and "that whenever we attempt to read the signs of the times it is helpful to listen to young people and the elderly." EG 51;108.

8  Nov 28, 2012. http://www.vatican.va/holy_father/benedict_xvi/audiences/2012/documents/hf_ben-xvi_aud_20121128_en.html

9  See more at: http://www.rtcc.org/2014/05/08/un-to-back-pope-francis-statement-on-human-ecology/#sthash.eTR9vtyV.dpuf

10  A few authors have explored these themes and tried to divine the next encyclical. See *America Magazine:* http://americamagazine.org/content/all-things/what-hope-pope-francis-first-encyclical and *Catholic Ecology:*

sence of the Pope's environmental message lies in returning to the Latin American Catholic roots of his thinking.[11] Here we must turn to Alberto Methol Ferré, known as "the Pope's philosopher."[12] He was one of the most important technical experts invited by the CELAM Bishops who drafted the Puebla and Medellin documents and also happened to be a close friend to Bergoglio.

Ferré identifies "libertine atheism" as the greatest enemy of faith in our times: "one cannot redeem libertine atheism's kernel of truth with an argumentative or dialectical procedure; much less can one do so by setting up prohibitions, raising alarms, dictating abstract rules. Libertine atheism is not an ideology, it is a practice. A practice must be opposed with another practice; a self-aware practice, of course, which means one that is equipped intellectually." Pope Francis is following this program very carefully by avoiding ideological battles and conflictive statements that can be absorbed into culture war rhetoric. He is rather proposing a positive practice of life; hence the car choice, house choice, clothes choice, kiss the baby, enjoy a mate—faith must engage the entire being.

The importance of combating libertine atheism with a practice also explains the emphasis the Pope attaches to popular piety[13]—a reality I find almost impossible to explain to Anglo-Americans.[14] Popular piety

---

http://catholicecology.blogspot.com/2014/01/seven-things-to-know-about-franciss.html

[11] While these ideas and their expressions such as popular piety are particularly important in Latin America, it does not mean that they are circumscribed to Latin American culture. In fact, the fact that Pope Francis has emphasized it so much in *Evangelii Gaudium* and as such directed at the universal Church suggests that this Latin American influence is a gift to the entire Church, and where each culture must find its own expressions.

[12] See: "El Papa y el Filosofo" and http://chiesa.espresso.repubblica.it/articolo/1350753?eng=y

[13] EG 122–126

[14] Mostly because there's basically no autochthonous frame of reference for popular piety. One exception is to be found in the Hispanic culture of northern New Mexico and southern Colorado, fruit of the northernmost Franciscan missions of the 18th century. Apart from this I know of no other

is the most public (and uncontrived and non-political) expression of faith—it is the popular outpouring of beings who believe. It is concrete proof that faith is everything, matters over everything, and is expressed in everything. Quoting the Latin American Bishops, Francis called it the "people's mysticism"[15] that has the "capacity of expressing faith in a complete language that overcomes rationalisms (song, image, gesture, color, dance); this Faith situated in time (feasts) and place (sanctuaries and temples)."[16] By nature it is not contestatory but celebratory, joyful and expressed in a total language. It is in its essence a practice of faith.

Hence we must look more towards environmental practices (intellectually equipped) rather than mere ideas and theories. I would not be surprised if Pope Francis accompanies the encyclical with programs or activities that deal with feeding the poor in the developed world and challenge the rich to change their wasteful habits. I could go on about other approaches to human ecology and the environment, but being true to Pope Francis' vision, I rather want to conclude by proposing a practice.

---

autochthonous Catholic cultural synthesis apart from imported impostations from other cultures that have died due to the assimilation of Catholics into Anglo-Protestant mainstream. Other Catholics have identified the importance of popular piety for American Catholicism, for examples see the efforts of Fr. Ivan Illich http://solidarityhall.org/ivan-illichs-politics-of-carnival/ and the devotion to San Gennaro in New York http://www.crisismagazine.com/2013/the-miracles-of-san-gennaro. To explain popular piety I sometimes I use the example: it is what a people close their streets and change their calendars for; in the USA for 10k races and political rallies; in Latin America for religious processions.

The problem of public expression of faith in the USA is not restricted to popular piety either. The arts are an entire field that struggles to find true Catholic expression as described in the fields of literature by Dana Gioia and in film by Barbara Nicolosi. In turn, these two authors offer Catholic alternatives that seek to evangelize the synthesis of American culture true to Francis' style and approach and their work is a beacon of hope. Read Gioia http://www.firstthings.com/article/2013/12/the-catholic-writer-today and Nicolosi http://churchofthemasses.blogspot.com/2014/04/a-christian-cinema-interview-with-av.html

[15] EG 124

[16] *El Verdadero Poder es el Servicio*, 314; Puebla 454

## The Camino

Inspired by messages of Puebla, Aparecida and the Pope, in the last six months I have embarked on an experiment and a dream that integrates popular piety and the environment: the "Camino de Chimayo." Creatio, the environmental non-profit I founded, has led four different groups (about 50 people total, both Catholics and non-Catholics) for weeklong walking pilgrimages in New Mexico. The dream is that the Camino de Chimayo could become the North American equivalent of the "Camino de Santiago" in Spain (a century old path walked by pilgrims across northern Spain averaging 10–15 miles a day for ten days to a month or more).

Central to the probable success of the Camino de Chimayo is its history and location. In the heart of America, the region of Northern New Mexico from Albuquerque to the San Luis Valley in Colorado reflects a unique living synthesis of faith and culture. There, people are proudly American while at the same time most comfortable speaking Spanish (though today almost all are bilingual). Racially they are Hispanic mestizos (not Mexican and not Anglo). Most importantly, their identity lies in being Catholic—this is reflected in the celebration of saint feasts, processions, pilgrimages and many other traditions. Popular piety runs through the veins of this American Catholic people.

Furthermore, this entire area is surrounded by incredible natural and supernatural beauty. The natural beauty is seen in the high forests and snow capped peaks of Taos, as well as the fertile plains and rivers flowing through Española and Santa Fe, to the spectacular desert expanding to the west of Abiquiú. To walk 12–20 miles a day in this area is to experience freedom surrounded by Beauty and to be physically (it's a workout!) connected to earth, wind, fire and water. The natural scenery has nothing to envy Northern Spain, and the Franciscan evangelization of the 18th century guaranteed a chain of settlements within a days walking distance of each other.

If that were not enough, God has blessed this natural and human beauty with a supernatural gift in the miracle of Chimayo. In the early 19th century a poor farmer found a cross buried in his field. After removing the cross repeatedly only to find it miraculously returned to the same spot every morning, the Bishop decided to build a sanctuary around the blessed piece of land where to this day thousands of pilgrims (mostly locals) visit the Santuario every year. The Santuario contains the history, tradition and divine blessing of a true pilgrims destination. God blessed this land, and it is a treasure waiting to be found.

Therefore, I want to invite anyone—Catholic or not, young and old, rich and poor, sad and joyful, weak and strong, simple and sophisticated, busy and lazy—to be a pilgrim. The Camino de Chimayo is still very primitive in its infrastructure, so some previous planning and co-ordination needs to go into it beforehand.[17] For Creatio, the Camino de Chimayo has become our flagship activity, and I (or one of our guides) would be delighted to walk the Camino with you. Of course there are many other ways of putting Francis' message into practice; pilgrimage is only one example. But if the Camino is something that appeals to you, or you have no other better idea of how to put the Pope's message into practice, then in Francis' fashion, pick up the phone, send an email or tweet, but whatever you do, "go out!" Invite your friends, family, random people or join a group. "I want a mess in the dioceses! I want people to go out! I want the Church to go out to the street!" Let's start walking!

---

[17] You can contact the Santuario and they will be happy to coordinate, or you can contact me directly.

Ricardo Simmonds is a consecrated layman in the Sodalitium Christianae Vitae, a religious order founded in Peru. Originally from São Paulo, Brazil, Ricardo studied at Bowdoin College and subsequently obtained a Master's of Science degree in Environmental Studies from CU Boulder. Currently he is the Director of Penn Newman Center in Philadelphia. He is the founder of Creatio, a Catholic Environmental non-profit, and an international speaker on Catholic environmentalism. He has produced a 13-episode documentary on the environment for EWTN, and published *Truth and Climate Change: Pragmatist Truth Confronted by Habermas and Ratzinger in the Context of Climate Change* (Lambert) in 2013.

# An Open Letter to Pope Francis on the Ethical Economy

*Dear Pope Francis,*

I write to you as a cultural Catholic moved by admiration for the Christian values and how they have been embodied by social change activists such as Ivan Illich, E. F. Schumacher, Paulo Freire, and profound and provocative thinkers such as Marshall McLuhan and Bruno Latour.

I write to you as someone who has been honoured twice by invitations from the Pontifical Academy of Social Sciences, where I learned about the beautiful and balanced set of ideas that are the Social Doctrine of the Catholic Church and could interact with many interesting Catholic-inspired thinkers, from different sides of the political spectrum, yet open to each other's ideas in a spirit of brotherhood and sisterhood.

I write to you as well as an admirer of the cooperativism that is inspired by the social doctrine, such as the cooperative network of Mondragon, the ideas of Stefano Zamagni and many others.

I write to you as the founder of the Foundation for Peer to Peer Alternatives, and one of the founding partners of the Commons Strategies group, as someone who is deeply connected with emerging new productive practices based on peer to peer relationships, the creation of common pools of knowledge for the benefit of the whole of humanity, and of sharing economy practices that are based on the re-use of many idle resources that could benefit more citizens while lightening the load of humanity on our planet.

Finally, I write to you as the research coordinator of an ambitious transition project in Ecuador, which is advising the public authorities on moving towards a society and economy that is fully based on shared knowledge (floksociety.org).

In this context, I am of course very, very heartened by the recent statements of your Holiness about the need to care for the poor and weak, and to be mindful of the excesses of capitalism, but also from authoritarian collectivism.

I am aware of the key role that the Catholic Church has played in the moral economy of the Middle Ages, and how many Catholics, individually or collectively as members of Congregations and Catholic social movements, are engaged for the common good. I am inspired by historical examples such as the Banks of Piety of the Dominicans, which lend money without interest to the poor, and drove out usury-driven banking from their territories.

Yet, as many humans, I am also concerned about our human future. We presently live in a system which believes natural resources are infinite, and we are destroying the very eco-systems on which we depend; and the same system believes that knowledge that could benefit humanity should be restricted and kept artificially scarce, through intellectual property restrictions that slow down innovation, hide solutions until they are believed to be profitable, and sell vital medicines at inflated prices, amongst many other issues.

But I am also heartened by the emergence of new modes of creating and distributing value, and on the many peer-based and commons-oriented communities that are mutualizing knowledge, so that it can benefit all; and mutualizing physical infrastructures and resources, so that we may step lighter on the planet. These emergent movements and practices are vital for the future of our planet, and I strongly believe they need your help! At the end of the era of the Roman Empire, it was the Catholic monks, who mutualized both material infrastructure and knowledge, and functioned as European-wide open design communities, and were crucial in reviving European societies.

The Catholic Church, despite the difficulties due to secularization in Western countries, still has many vital resources. Sometimes, these resources are sold to the marketplace, which may use these in inappropriate ways, such as for examples using abandoned churches and monasteries for commercial purposes, for hotels and entertainment venues, but also including sometimes directly related to real-estate speculation.

At the same time, the younger generations of people, and I believe we have a beautiful generation that is concerned and engaged with the common good, are willing to create a new type of community, where work and resources are mutualized, and where they use their personal skills and resources, to work for the common good, through projects associated with social entrepreneurship, fair trade, peer production and the creation of vital commons of knowledge, code and design which are made universally available for all who need them. There are already quite a number of makerspaces, hackerspaces, co-working spaces and open manufacturing centers for open and sustainable technologies, but we need many more of them, and the reality of real-estate speculation makes many projects unnecessarily difficult to realize.

Indeed, this vital movement of humanity's young (and not so young) is in search of common places where they can engage in meaningful activities for the common good, yet, the reality of the current economy often means they are precarious, they cannot afford urban rents that are driven by real estate speculation, and often real estate prices make the mutualization of the workplace a very difficult endeavour.

Some of our friends want to go further and have already taken on monastery projects to revitalize our world with ecumenical projects such as the "unMonastery" project in Matera, Italy.

The Gorton Monastery, previously a Franciscan church and friary, in a deprived neighbourhood of Manchester, England. Deconsecrated and left by the Church, it was abandoned and devastated by the weather, theft and vandalism. It has since been restored by the Monastery of St. Francis and Gorton Trust, and once again brings Franciscan values to its community. The recently established

Monastery Foundation is leading in thought and action to support personal and organisational transition: the move from old ways of working and living to those required for today and tomorrow.

Another one is the Uniting Church's congregation known as the "Augustine Centre," which has been active for many years in the personal development and creative expression fields; it is now known as the Habitat Centre for Spirituality and has hosted the Borderlands Co-operative for the last twelve years. Together they have created a holistic post-graduate course of education called the "OASES Graduate School," offering a Master's Degree in Sustainability and Social Change, based on the understanding that education needs to be integrative of many disciplines and that it needs to lead to the transformation of all our ways of living and being. An accompanying range of other events, short courses and activities have been created, the place now becoming known for its ecological and social engagement.

These new practices are recreating the moral economy of the future, and could learn from the moral economy of the past, when the Church played such a vital role. On the other hand, by engaging with these vital forces that are changing our society and civilization, the Church would also learn about the new spiritual needs that are co-emerging from these practices.

So the new movement would benefit from your assistance, and I am therefore making this proposal and appeal.

Why not think about the repurposing of unused Church property, for precisely the recreation of a moral and ethical economy? Why not create mechanisms for the creation of common hackerspaces, makerspaces, co-working spaces, where the common endeavours can take place in a meaningful and spiritualized space?

My hope is that the forces of the Catholic Church may start thinking about using resources to assist the great and necessary transformation that is starting to take place today.

As my Catholic friend and ethical investor Dr. Johnny Spangenberg writes, warning of humanity's mistaken admiration for false gods:

We create catastrophic climate risk and trigger natural disaster by destroying the very ecosystems on which we depend—all in the name of the worldly gods of GDP & EBITDA growth and with disregard for the needs of the poor or vulnerable ecosystems. KeyStone XL Pipeline is a recent example of such a controversial megaproject in which the long-run welfare of the human race is sacrificed for short-term economic interest....

Dr. Spangenberg also mentions a way forward which is similar to the proposed approach of mutualized working spaces, but expanded to the scale of a village:

> The Regen-Villages—an innovative collaboration between Stanford University, Danish Technical University, and the University of Malaysia Pahang (amongst others)—aim to rapidly create modern and comfortable integrated villages around the world that can feed and power themselves. As an urgent call to action to combat economic inequality, RV focus is on thriving rural and sub-urban villages that will run on renewable energy and high-yield organic food production, creating a surplus for thriving, self-sustaining communities. RV also brings curriculum into these villages, while fostering the export of innovation and ingenuity out of these villages.

Therefore, we believe that the transformation discussed above, which requires spaces for meaningful and sustainable work, is vital to save our planet and humanity, and vital for the future of the Church.

We are, of course, not in the position to demand anything, this is not our purpose, but we humbly suggest starting a dialogue on how the Church can support the forces for practical and moral regeneration of our failing economic system. One of our key concerns and proposals would be to find a proper purpose for the religious buildings that are presently unused, and we believe that creating meaning collective workplaces is one of these."

We are very thankful for any attention that this letter may generate,

*Michel Bauwens,*

Commons Strategies Group and P2P Foundation

The general idea and proposition in this letter are endorsed by the following groups and individuals:

- David Bollier and Silke Helfrich
  Commons Strategies Group, co-editors of *The Wealth of the Commons* (Levellers Press, 2012).

- Hasnah Ismail
  Senior Consultant Fellow, Putra Business School & Director, Might-Meteor Advanced Manufacturing, Kuala Lumpur.

- James Ehrlich
  Senior Technologist, Stanford University, Human-Sciences and Technologies Advanced Research Institute (H-STAR), Stanford.

- Giovanni Luchetti
  Representative of Harvard Business Review, World Investment News, New York.

- Marco Fioretti
  Founder of the Catholic free software/digital rights movement Elèutheros.

- Francois Houtart
  Fundación Indígena/IAEN, Quito.

- Johnny Spangenberg
  CEO & Founder, GeoSayang ClimateRiskBonds, New York.

Michel Bauwens, an occasional invitee of the Pontifical Academy of Social Sciences, is the founder of the P2P Foundation, which studies and promotes peer production, peer governance and peer property modalities. He recently crafted the Commons Transition Plan for Ecuador. He lives in Chiang Mai, Thailand.

# CITY

# Toward the New
# Economy of Inclusion

Prophets tend to appear when and where they are most needed. So it is altogether appropriate that Pope Francis arrived on the scene in the immediate aftermath of the worst global economic crisis since the Great Depression, at a time of great anxiety and uncertainty in which the very economic foundations of the modern economy are being called into question.

The pope's denunciation of the pathologies underlying our global economic system is well known at this stage. We can hear his indictment ringing in our ears:

> Inequality is the root of social ills. We also have to say "thou shalt not" to an economy of exclusion and inequality—such an economy kills. The culture of prosperity deadens us. The thirst for power and possessions knows no limits. The excluded are still waiting. Men and women are sacrificed to the idols of profit and consumption. People are disposed of, as if they were trash. In this world of globalization, we have fallen into a globalization of indifference. The worship of the golden calf of old has found a new and heartless image in

the cult of money. We can no longer trust in the unseen forces and the invisible hand of the market.

These words are packed with power, passion, and prophecy. From the perspective of Catholic social teaching, of course, none of this is new. What is new is the tone, the stridency, the urgency of the call for a major economic course correction—and a major conversion.

## What Went Wrong With Economics?

I am an economist. I trained as an economist, and have worked in that field for many years now. But it has become increasingly clear to me that something has really gone awry with the practice of economics. It has veered off course in a rather dramatic fashion.

Economics was once a branch of moral philosophy, concerned with virtue and human flourishing. It is unrecognizable as such today. What went wrong?

I suppose we must start at the beginning, and that directs us to the core tenet of the Enlightenment—the voluntarist elevation of the supremacy of the individual, his autonomy and freedom from external coercion. This principle defines the modern world, and it defines modern economics—especially through the idea that what motivates the individual is self-interest alone.

And here, many point the finger at Adam Smith. This certainly makes a fair amount of sense. Smith is justifiably regarded as the godfather of modern economics, given his belief that self-interest trumps benevolence in market exchange. Yet Smith was unwilling to fully reject the old ways. His main work was not the *Wealth of Nations,* but rather the *Theory of Moral Sentiments,* which is primarily about living a virtuous life. He certainly parted company with people like Bernard Mandeville who relished in private vice leading to public virtue.

For a thorough answer to the question of what went wrong, though, we need to look to another child of the Enlightenment project—to utilitarianism, the idea that human beings are guided only by their desire to maximize pleasure and minimize pain. With a degree of confidence typical of the Enlightenment, Jeremy Bentham believed that we could maximize the social welfare of the society as a whole—the greatest happiness of the greatest number. What we might need to do to get there, however, can take us to some dark places.

Bentham also developed the notion of diminishing marginal utility—the idea that an extra dollar brings more utility to a poor person than a rich person. As many have noted, if you take this to its logical conclusion, it not only provides a cogent argument for redistribution, but can indeed be used to justify complete equality. Bentham's consequentialism certainly had horrendous implications for human life and dignity, but there was nonetheless a subversive element contained within it.

Yet Bentham glossed over the radical implications of his philosophy, and it was completely ruled out by the next generation of utilitarians, including Vilfredo Pareto, who made an enormous contribution to the development of modern economics. Like others at the time, Pareto sought to correct the monstrously consequentialist ethos of pure utilitarianism, but his method involved prohibiting any interpersonal comparisons of utility whatsoever. People are different, he argued, so it is simply not possible to assess their relative happiness based on some objective yardstick.

Pareto's big insight was his idea that a person could maximize their individual utility through voluntary exchanges in a free market. As long as there are mutually beneficial trades to be made, then the outcome is not efficient. It becomes efficient—*Pareto efficient* or *Pareto optimal*—when nobody can be made any better off without making somebody else worse off. Today, this is still the standard framework for economists to assess efficiency. It is the space where utility meets autonomy.

Notice what this means. The Benthamite rationale for redistribution is now ruled out completely. To take an extreme example: taking a dollar from a billionaire to give to somebody starving to death cannot be defended. I am not saying that economists would actually hold this position. They would merely say that it would violate the Pareto criterion, and would require some other justification, based on a trade-off between efficiency and equity. But the very dominance of Pareto optimality as a way of valuing economic outcomes is telling.

From this came the two fundamental theorems of welfare economics. Developed in the 20th century with deep mathematical rigor, these theorems meld decisively the utilitarianism ethos with the virtues of a free market economy. The first theorem says that the competitive free market is always Pareto efficient. The second says that any Pareto efficient allocation can be reached through the magic of the market. Thus was born general equilibrium economics: consumers maximize utility (identified with material possessions), firms maximize profits, and the great invisible hand of the free market will guide all to the best possible outcome.

Such a framework has no use for distributional issues—the issues that taxed the virtue ethicists of yore as well as the great classical economists like Smith, Ricardo, and Marx. Distributive justice, once a core concern, was simply written off. All that mattered now was commutative justice, the justice of contracts and exchange. Why? Because market prices were deemed fair and just. This includes the price of factors of production—including labor—whose returns depend on their marginal products, reflecting their economic contribution.

Of course, for the market to reach this virtuous outcome, it needs to be unconstrained by external forces. So economics, although rooted in ends-based utilitarianism, became extremely comfortable with rights-based notions of economic freedom and autonomy—with the classical liberal doctrine of *laissez-faire* and even the more extreme self-ownership doctrine of the libertarians. Pareto and the neo-utilitarians started this mind meld, but it grew stronger over time.

This was especially true in the Anglo-Saxon world, which makes sense given the particular form the Enlightenment took in these regions. In the United States in particular, it also reflects the Calvinist heritage, with material success interpreted as a sign of divine favor. Europe proved more resistant in this regard, given its far deeper communitarian roots—roots that go back to what was once known as Christendom.

Let me step back for a moment and note that the picture I have painted contains some elements of caricature. Every economist worth her salt understands the strict conditions needed for the market to be efficient. Everybody knows about the multiple ways markets can fail.

So most would accept a role for the state, at least in theory. They would accept the idea of public goods, like infrastructure and education, which the market does not do a good job in providing. They would understand the consequences of negative externalities, the idea that markets do not take social costs into account—environmental degradation being the leading example. They would acknowledge that limited and asymmetric information stops the market from working well, as so often happens in areas like healthcare and finance.

Going even further, most economists would also recognize that efficiency cannot be the only goal of the economic system, and must therefore be tempered with equity concerns, especially by supporting an element of redistribution. They would likely support basic safety nets to protect people from falling through the cracks that inevitably appear in the structure of every market economy.

Yet we should not play down the damage done by this strange stepchild of utilitarianism and classical liberalism. Its clarity and elegance proved too alluring. It led to such notions as the efficient market hypothesis, the idea that self-interest makes sure that financial markets are always efficient—which in turn was used to justify imprudent financial sector deregulation. It gave rise to the idea that the sole goal of business is to maximize profits, which gives license to run roughshod over other stakeholders like workers, suppliers, the environment, and society as a whole. It cheered on a form of hyper-commercialism that wallowed in excess and short-term pleasure. And it led to a neglect of distributional issues, moving this from the realm of economics to the realm of politics.

## The Pathologies of the Modern Economic System

In short, it gave rise to the pathologies of the modern economy. And these pathologies run deep indeed. As Thomas Piketty has shown, the modern capitalist economy contains an important design flaw, one that we ignore at our peril—an inbuilt tendency toward heightened inequality, leading to all kinds of dysfunctions and imbalances.

If we cannot see this, it is because we are blinded by the unique achievements of the postwar era—a period of remarkable economic strength combined with low inequality. As Piketty tells it, this period was really a temporary deviation from a longer-term tendency toward greater inequality. What happened is that the unprecedented catastrophes of the last century—two world wars and the Great Depression—led to a great leveling in society, a leveling abetted by policies designed to instill a sense of social solidarity in a time of crisis. This ethos carried through to the postwar period as high levels of regulation, worker protection, and taxation made sure that the inevitable spurt in growth as the world emerged from crisis was both safer and more inclusive than before.

This might be a fondly remembered golden age, but it did not last long. By the 1970s, it was already on its last legs. The postwar growth spurt was petering out. At the same time, a sequence of economic crises created a search for new solutions, which were actually rather old solutions. There was a noticeable shift away from the postwar idea of public and private sector in partnership, and more toward an older and purer laissez-faire model—more deregulation and less redistribution. The idea that the market needed to be tempered by the state increasingly fell out of fashion. Not surprisingly, this new wave began in the Anglo-Saxon countries, but it soon spread far and wide.

The results of this experiment are in, and they are not pretty. Yes, the market economy scored some impressive wins over the past few decades—including by lifting hundreds of millions of people out of poverty. But these gains were predominantly in places like India and China, countries with huge populations previously stuck in closed and collectivist economic systems. Yes, there have also been gains in reducing extreme poverty elsewhere, including in Africa, and these gains have been impressive. But this reflects a concerted policy effort to advance human development—such as through the Millennium Development Goals—rather than the magic of the free market. Overall, there is very little correlation between limited state intervention and economic success.

The story is even more stark among the advanced economies, especially in "libertarian ground zero" of the United States. Despite the promises of the supply-siders and the free market zealots, economic productivity—the key driver of longer-term economic growth—did not budge. Long-term economic growth was no higher than in the past. What did move was economic inequality—sharply upwards. Economic growth began to benefit the top echelons of society while real wages stagnated. Inequality was on the rise anyway from the twin forces of technology and globalization, but the rollback of the state made this a lot worse.

The renewed emphasis on the virtues of the market unleashed a tidal wave of greed. This led to a shattering of the social norms supporting solidarity, as it became more and more acceptable to open up huge income gaps between the top and everyone else, gaps that would have been regarded as tawdry and imprudent in the postwar era. It also led to a far greater acceptance of cutting ethical corners in pursuit of profit, especially in the world of finance. This in turn led to a huge increase in economic fragility, culminating in the worst global economic crisis since the Great Depression—a crisis with distinct roots in the economic philosophy of the past quarter century.

Why should worry so much about this? Because at a basic level, inequality is synonymous with exclusion, and an economy of exclusion is ultimately a failed economy. It prevents people from fully participating and from developing their true potential—because they lack basic healthcare, education, skills, opportunities, or finance. This creates a vicious cycle as the poor are stuck in a trap of exclusion.

It is therefore not surprising that inequality stunts social mobility. There is a striking statistical association between high inequality and low intergenerational mobility across countries. Known as the "Great Gatsby curve," this shows clearly that any nostalgia for an "American dream" is tied to a unique postwar period that has long past.

The pathologies run deeper still. In more unequal societies, we find lower levels of happiness, contentment, and trust. As Richard Wilkinson and Kate Pickett have demonstrated, higher levels of inequality are associated with a broad array of social maladies—pervasive health problems; earlier death; more violence, criminality and drug use;

greater incidence of mental illness; higher levels of insecurity and indebtedness.

In the United States, the rise in inequality tracks neatly with the fall in social capital over the past few decades. As people drift apart in incomes, opportunities, and lifestyles, they will also drift apart in terms of social networks, shared interests, and common goals. The social glue that binds society together start to come undone. Civic virtue is replaced by an uncivil self-absorption. Globalization only makes things worse, with less connection and more exclusion. So does financialization—when elites make money more and more from the world of finance, they grow further and further apart from the economy inhabited by the majority.

In these starkly unequal societies, the poor are pushed to the far fringes of society, and not seen at all. Pope Francis knows this well, as Latin America is one of the world's most unequal regions. But we see this more and more in the United States too—the poor are no longer seen as common citizens in need of a helping hand, but as undeserving parasites—the vicious "takers" rather than the virtuous "makers." America's twin legacies of Calvinism and institutionalized racism only add fuel to these harsh flames.

At the other end of the scale, depleted social capital can lead to a culture of dependency. With no real sense of belonging or connection to wider society, people will simply retreat further into enclaves of exclusion—another vicious cycle.

There is a political dimension to all of this too, of course. In more unequal societies, the rich are more likely to dominate the political system, and enact policies to protect their privilege. This has always been clear in Latin America, and it is increasingly clear in the United States. Think about the declining real minimum wage, the attack on collective bargaining rights, the rollback of financial regulations, the erosion of the social safety net, the lax tax treatment of unearned income, and the huge drops in top income tax rates. Despite the rhetoric, none of this really benefits the economy, and in actual fact does a lot of harm.

The situation has become so bad that an influential study claimed that the United States was now more of an oligarchy than a democracy. This might not be too surprising, but it is still shocking.

When elites have a dwindling stake in a common future, decisions take on a far greater short-term dimension. They care more about the fleeting financial returns of today than the sustainable economy of tomorrow. Corporate profits are at record highs today, but the captains of finance are using that money not to invest in people or productive capacity, but to buy back shares and boost financial returns—self-interest over social benefit. In such an environment, even charity and philanthropy can become a mask for self-centered narcissism—I help the people I desire to help on my own terms in return for lot of social approval.

Inequality, of course, provides a macabre rationale for this short-termism. With wages and incomes stuck in the mud, companies are naturally uncertain about future demand for their products—and so divert resources toward activities that make inequality even worse. It is yet another vicious cycle.

## A New Path

So what can be done about all of this? There is clearly a role for government policy. The dysfunctions of the market have been reined in before, and they can be again. They *must* be again. But this will not be enough. We must go deeper, a lot deeper.

Put it this way: it's not just that things took a wrong turn because Reagan and Thatcher read too much Friedman and Hayek, although this is surely part of it. We must also acknowledge that things took a wrong turn centuries earlier, when modern economics took a splash of individualism and a dash of utilitarianism, coalescing into the dominant orthodoxy of today. Despite all the hot air over the size and reach of government, this orthodoxy is rarely questioned.

Yet it must be questioned, because its basic underlying assumptions—self-interest, autonomy, and a narrow concern for the accumulation of material goods—are quite simply wrong. They do not reflect human nature—either *as it is* or *as it should be*. As long as we cling to these assumptions, we are led down a blind ally.

In reality, human beings are primarily social and cooperative, not atomistic and self-centered. Aristotle was surely right—we are social animals through and through. The theologians can give us deeper insights: we are fundamentally relational persons, not autonomous individuals, finding meaning and purpose in encounter and collaboration.

What really stands out is the importance of fairness, trust, and cooperation. These principles are deeply rooted within us. We can see this from psychology, neuroscience, and evolutionary biology. Just ask any child who is given even slightly less of something than his or her sibling! But the same is true for adults. We have a lot of experimental evidence back this up.

As just one example, consider the famous ultimatum game—A is asked to divide a fixed sum (say $100) between herself and another player, B. B can either accept, in which case the division takes place as agreed, or reject, in which case both get nothing. Now, the logic of self-interest that underlies Pareto efficiency suggests that A offers B the smallest amount possible, say $1. If B acted like a true *homo economicus,* he would accept the offer, as he is better off than before. But this doesn't happen. Neither does A act like a self-interested automaton. As Samuel Bowles has shown, in experiments all across the world, the vast majority of proposers offer between 40 and 50 percent of the pie, and offers less than 20 percent are typically rejected. The bottom line is that people loath unfairness and are willing to incur a cost to punish people who are seen as unfair. It is small wonder that inequality creates such social dysfunction.

From this perspective, the true guiding principle of economics is less self-interest than reciprocity—cooperation for mutual benefit, letting fraternity add seasoning to our economic encounters. This means foregoing the maximum benefit to ourselves in order to give a benefit to others, trusting that such a blessing will be returned. As Luigino Bruni and Stefano Zemagni put it, reciprocity is the golden rule of the market, as economics is really the domain of common advantage.

*Homo reciprocans* provides a far better description of human nature than *homo economicus.*

This is not some fanciful utopianism. *Homo reciprocans* can actually deliver a stronger and healthier economy. Fraternity pays off. It boosts trust and social capital, the lifeblood of a healthy economy. It moves us away from the curse of the modern business economy—the belief that the only goal is to maximize financial value. It reduces exclusion and inequality and encourages participation. It promotes a more trusting and harmonious relationship between employers and workers, which is good for productivity. It instills a sense of common purpose and common destiny—and it promotes the common good.

Reciprocity is the perfect antidote to the bifurcated life of *homo economicus*—the idea that benevolent and social Dr. Jekyll must turn into a cold and calculating Mr. Hyde to survive in a Darwinian economy. *Homo reciprocans* can make us whole again, by bringing all-important human relationships into the heart of economic life, rather than leaving them at the door.

It should come as no surprise, therefore, that reciprocity is also a boon for happiness and contentment. As social beings, we know that relationality is one of the keys to happiness—this is a key finding of behavioral economists like Daniel Kahneman. Psychological studies show the same thing. Once people have reached a certain threshold of income to live comfortably, money no longer buys happiness.

Specifically, Luigino Bruni links happiness to a class of goods known as "relational goods," goods that can only be enjoyed if shared reciprocally, where the source of the good lies in the relationship itself. The problem lies when rising income crowds out these valued relationships, especially through long working hours and the atomization of the market economy. It is simply not the case that we maximize our utility through possession and consumption. Gross domestic product simply cannot account for the value of our human relationships.

For Bruni, if we throw out relationships in favor an the impersonal market, then we lose part of what it means to be human. He faults Adam Smith here—Smith saw the impersonal marketplace as a blessed escape from the exploitative and hierarchical relationships of the time. But by thinking of the market as a relation-free zone, he basically threw the baby out with the bathwater.

There is another dimension to all of this, another design flaw in *homo economicus*. We are creatures of reciprocity, but we are also creatures of teleology, finding meaning and happiness in a sense of purpose. We find fulfillment in reaching our goals, realizing our potential, finding our vocation—always within the social context, the communal life. In turn, we reach our goals by cultivating virtue, and this requires practice. There is a dynamic context here that is entirely absent from emphasis of modern economics on fixed tastes and preferences. It is what we do, not how much we spend, that really matters. It is ultimately, as Aristotle taught us, about *eudaimonia*—human flourishing, or becoming who we are meant to be.

This is one reason why inequality and the economy of exclusion prove so harmful. They not only prevent a person from improving their material lot in life, but also from fulfilling their true potential. Inequality cuts off purpose and cuts off cooperation—a devastating double blow.

In this context, of course, virtue is intrinsically linked to happiness. As Jeffrey Sachs noted in last year's *World Happiness Report*, the old idea of happiness—not just from Aristotle but also from the Buddhist philosophy in the east—came from living the "good life" imbued with the proper virtues. It goes without saying that happiness in this context is very different from the pleasure seeking of the utilitarians, or—in its modern incarnation—maximizing the consumption of material goods.

As Aristotle said himself, "wealth is evidently not the good we are seeking; for it is merely useful and for the sake of something else." Money cannot ultimately bring happiness. Material goods ultimately cannot satisfy. Profit cannot be the ultimate end of business, either. Business also has a goal, a purpose—providing a genuine benefit for people—and this purpose requires virtue. As the Vatican's *Vocation of the Business Leader* puts it, it must produce goods that are truly good and services that truly serve. And the virtue needed for this vision goes far beyond the minimal standards of personal honesty, obeying the rules, or even engaging in philanthropy.

If we look at it from this angle, it is not hard to see what went wrong. By substituting narrow materialism for expansive human flourishing, the utilitarian ethos gives us the wrong end-point. And by prioritizing the right over the good—the *individual* right over the *common* good—the mindset of economic freedom unmoors us from any real sense of purpose. It sets us out on a path with a blindfold on. We are given no idea of where we are going or how to get there. And to add insult to injury, we are discouraged from cooperating with other blindfolded people. No wonder we go astray so often.

A key conclusion here is that virtue is not only the route to personal wellbeing, but also to the wellbeing of the entire economy. A greater focus on virtue tied to purpose would fix some of the maladies of the modern economy. It would lead to less exclusion and more innovation, less excess and more moderation, less focus on short-term financial gain and more focus on long-term sustainability. We have seen too many examples of negative habituation—the pervasive acceptance that the economics world is an ethics-free wild west. This is dysfunctional. It is time to turn it around completely, and create a true "virtuous" cycle—in accord with our true nature.

## Conclusion

My main conclusion is that we need a radical transformation of how we approach our economic interactions, one more in accord with human nature and human motivation than the dominant paradigm of the Enlightenment. There is a sense of urgency about all of this. We are already seeing the expansion of inequality and a globalized economy of exclusion. In the years ahead, we will also be running faster and faster into the wall of sustainability, as we run up against the natural boundaries of our precious planet—especially from the merciless march of climate change.

The task ahead is a momentous one. It is not a task for government alone, although government must of course play an indispensible role. But so must private business, and indeed all global citizens. For instead of assuming that private vice leads to public virtue, and instead of assuming a bifurcation between the values of the market and the values of civil society, we need a fusing of private and public virtue, knowing that such a fusion can multiply our collective blessings.

The good news is that we have a roadmap for a better economic vision. I am thinking of the roadmap offered by Catholic social teaching with its foundational principle of the dignity of every person and its abiding commitment to the common good of all people. Yes, this is rooted in the theology of the Catholic Church, but I believe it can appeal to all peoples from all traditions—because it is based on who we are as human beings, and who we yearn to be.

One thing is for certain: we cannot continue on our present path. Such a path is neither sustainable nor is it ultimately rewarding. This is why the prophetic voice of Pope Francis is so important today. Let us heed it.

 Tony Annett has a B.A. and an M.Litt from Trinity College Dublin, and a Ph.D. in economics from Columbia University. He is currently a Climate Change and Sustainable Development Advisor at the Earth Institute at Columbia University, and he also works with Religions for Peace in this position. Prior to this, he worked at the International Monetary Fund for sixteen years, including as speechwriter for two successive Managing Directors, Dominique Strauss-Kahn and Christine Lagarde. He is also a Knight Commander of the Equestrian Order of the Holy Sepulchre of Jerusalem.

# The Great Divide

Well into the second year of Pope Francis' papacy we reflect on how the effects of this seismic shift in Catholic leadership—both the unprecedented resignation of Pope Benedict and the selection of a pontiff from the global south—affects the church throughout the world. In my context of the Catholic Church in the United States I see a number of ways in which clear lines or divisions are drawn in a longstanding cultural battle with ecclesial, theological, and ethical consequences. The papacy of Francis brings to the fore a division in the U.S. Catholic church along the lines of how we have come to understand the preferential option for the poor in the U.S. context. This division is not new. Historically, we have preferred our U.S. brand of Catholicism to be more in sync with national interests—economic, cultural, social, political—than in tension with them.

Two stories illustrate this divide for me. During the presidential election of 2012 the U.S. saw the historical occasion of having two Roman Catholic vice-presidential candidates. However, Senator Paul Ryan and now Vice-President Joe Biden had very different views of how their Catholic faith informed their sense of political responsibility, their definition of the common good, and the role of government in establishing, nourishing, and protecting it.

Besides differences in their read on the common good—a central tenet of Catholic social thought (CST)—they also differed significantly on how to interpret other key elements of CST, with clear implications on their policy agendas as reflected during their campaigns.[1] Specifically, there was a stark contradiction between their vastly different visions of solidarity and subsidiarity.[2] What stood out for me during the run up to the election were not the widely divergent versions of these two concepts. Rather, I was astounded at the lack of effort put by the leadership of the church to provide any clarity to the faithful on this matter, clearly affecting our thought and decision making as an electorate. A number of U.S. Catholic theologians saw it pertinent to provide clarification on the points in which the Ryan budget proposal at the time was in distinct contradiction of several CST principles;[3] "On All of Our Shoulders: A Catholic Call to Protect the Endangered Common Good" is also available online.[4]

As a result of this very contentious conversation on Catholic teaching and public policy in the U.S., carried out in ways that I found highly unhelpful, I established the Facebook page "Catholic Social Thought, Politics, and the Public Square,"[5] a place where open conversation on Catholic teaching and the public square could be encouraged, supported by the expertise of Catholic ethicists and theologians around the globe. With over 1,500 members, this page illustrates the Ryan/Biden divide of 2012 in the ongoing and sometimes contentious debates among people of faith from all walks of life, trying to answer questions regarding human rights, the common good, free will, the role of government, love of neighbor, and, most importantly, the option for the poor. Specifically, conversations in this page try to address how best to advocate for and enact policies addressing issues throughout the spec-

---

1  You may find a helpful glossary of key terms and principles of Catholic social thought at
   http://www.catholicsocialteaching.org.uk/principles/glossary/.

2  http://www.ncregister.com/daily-news/rep.-ryan-we-have-pursued-solidarity-but-abused-subsidiarity. See also: http://americamagazine.org/node/150554

3  http://www.faithinpubliclife.org/newsroom/press/catholic-leaders-to-rep-paul-ryan-stop-distorting-church-teaching-to-justify-immoral-budget/

4  http://www.onourshoulders.org/

5  https://www.facebook.com/groups/369868266420381/

trum of life, including poverty. Strong disagreements abound, especially as to how Christians are to promote the well-being of the poor within the context of a liberal capitalist democracy.

The second insight comes from my revisiting the U.S. Bishops' 1986 pastoral letter "Economic Justice for All"[6] on its 25th anniversary. This opportunity caused me to take a critical look at a document that I have used again and again in coursework as an example of a Catholic critique of the economy and the ways it participates in, sustains, and even creates conditions of injustice. However, this time around I simply asked the question "who is still missing?" This led me to discover that both the 1986 document, as well as the 1995 pastoral message "A Decade After 'Economic Justice for All': Continuing Principles, Changing Context, New Challenges,"[7] do not adequately speak to the way our economy requires a migrant, largely undocumented labor force.

In an essay reflecting on this insight I suggest that a key reason why migrant labor, 1980s sanctuary movement, the United Farm Workers grape boycott, or other migrant labor movements, do not make it into either one of these documents is the intrinsic and almost wholesale support of the bishops for the American experiment.[8] Since its origins, Christian support for the constitutional, human rights centered, democratic and capitalist project of the United States as a nation has been part and parcel of Christian life in this country. While there are periods in U.S. history during which some Christian churches stood in resistance to particular policies or practices (for example during the anti-slavery or the civil rights movement), we have for the most part offered our support and blessing to the American project. While recognizing its still incomplete commitments to freedom and equal worth and oppor-

---

6  http://www.usccb.org/upload/economic_justice_for_all.pdf

7  http://www.usccb.org/issues-and-action/human-life-and-dignity/global-issues/trade/upload/a-decade-after-economic-justice-for-all-1995-11.pdf

8  María Teresa Dávila, "Who is still missing? Economic Justice and Immigrant Justice," in *The Almighty and the Dollar: Reflections on Economic Justice for All*, edited by Mark Allman (Winona, MN: Anselm Academic, 2012), 214–227.

tunity (something the bishops acknowledged in 1986), U.S.-style democratic capitalism is perceived as the political vehicle through which the central elements of the Christian vision of the human person and life in society can be achieved and sustained.

I believe these stories highlight two critical elements of Catholic life in the U.S., vis-à-vis engagement with the public square. First, for the most part Catholics in the U.S. have joined other mainline Protestant churches in non-critical support of our political and economic systems. Second, because a deeper religious critique of the American experiment is not available from church leadership, the faithful placing their faith in conversation with public life are left on their own to bicker about how best to tweak or change the policies they perceive as counter to Christian life. Without guidance on how to have these critical conversations about policies and politics in a way that reflects both charity in engagement and unity around the central ethical concepts of human dignity, option for the poor, and the common good, these conversations are divisive, excluding of opposing views, and capitalized by both media and politicians in order to further their popularity and profit driven agendas.

## Pope Francis' Incarnational Approach

At the heart of the stories above is the historical unwillingness of the church to deal with the conflict experienced in human history, to authentically take the side of the victims this conflict creates, and address historically (culturally, politically, etc.) the dynamics that create conflict. I believe this is something that Pope Francis, in his approach, sensibilities, and grounding on the option for the poor understands and encourages in the local and the global church.

Francis' first acts as pontiff evoke for me what I describe as the preferential option for the poor as the incarnational principle of Divine love.9 That is, the option for the poor is that Christian principle by which we seek to concretely imitate God's act of becoming incarnate in our own poverty and humility as frail and mortal human beings

---

9 http://www.politicaltheology.com/blog/the-incarnational-principle-of-divine-love/

through acts of becoming present in transformative ways in the suffering of others. Washing the feet of inmates at a prison, saying mass among migrants at Lampedusa, stopping both at the wall of separation between Israel and Palestine and the Wailing Wall in Jerusalem—these are all acts of becoming incarnate in the suffering of the victims of historical conflict. In the face of these moments conflict is approached, not as a source of exclusionary positions or antagonistic political and media agendas, but as opportunities for accompaniment, embrace, and prayerful resistance of that which divides. The Pope's invitation to both the Israeli and Palestinian leaders to a joint prayer session[10] at the Vatican and its actual occasion is a visible and salient example of how Francis' engagement with conflict is driven by the demand to become fully present wherever conflict and strife causes human damage.

It is from this becoming incarnate in the suffering of others that conversations between faith and politics should begin. Perhaps it is Francis' Latin-American sensibility, marked by the scars of tyranny and repressive violence, his acquaintance with liberation theology, or a more populist hermeneutic typical of the Argentinian context that move him to engage with the world in a way that expresses presence and solidarity without appearing divisive.

The U.S. Catholic bishops' mass at the U.S./Mexico border[11] is an example that evokes Francis' sensibilities and praxis of becoming incarnate in the suffering of another for transformation. The act was criticized[12] as a politicization of the holy Eucharist by bringing it to such a politically charged location. But, like Francis' prayer day with the leaders from Israel and Palestine, the homily by Cardinal Sean O'Malley served to highlight the plight of victims in a yet-to-be-resolved conflict over immigration. Sidestepping partisan and divisive rhetoric,

---

[10] http://www.nytimes.com/2014/06/09/world/europe/pope-francis-holds-vatican-prayer-summit-with-israeli-and-palestinian-leaders.html?_r=0

[11] http://www.latimes.com/nation/la-na-bishops-immigration-20140402-story.html

[12] http://ncronline.org/blogs/distinctly-catholic/weigel-criticizes-omalley-bishops-over-border-mass

O'Malley was attentive to the humanity of those who suffer both in their home countries and through the perilous journey to cross the border.

## Seeing Differently in the Rubric "See-Judge-Act"

Partisan and ideological divisions in the U.S., within civil society and particularly within the churches, have reached a fever pitch with catastrophic consequences. A seemingly endless list of non-negotiables—some not at all related to basic doctrine—on which folks are unable to compromise or engage in conversation (same-sex marriage, government assistance, reproductive rights, immigration, free market economics) make it impossible to do as Francis has witnessed in his ministry. We are, in essence, unable to truly "see" where suffering and conflict are affecting real human beings who require Christian love in action. Therefore, our most basic rubric for engaging our faith in the world, "see-judge-act," is highly compromised.

When Francis' approach to and example of discipleship in action, grounded on the option for the poor, are described as an "agenda," the option for the poor as incarnational principle of Divine love is interpreted as an ideological bend, rather than a basic principle in Christian thought. The option for the poor as an incarnational principle requires that we shift or shake up the lenses through which we "see," to begin from the lived experience of those who suffer at the hands of human conflict, rather than beginning from the divisions, partisanship, and exclusionary rhetoric to which we have become committed before engaging in the hermeneutic of justice. The other two "legs" of the hermeneutic of justice—"judge" and "act"—depend heavily on where we begin in the "see" moment, and who we see with. The realm of the possible expands, Christian imagination is truly engaged, and a third way becomes a true unifying goal when we ground ourselves on incarnated, lived experience. From this perspective, the U.S. bishops' mass on the U.S.-Mexico border is a first act of being with while trying to overcome the divisiveness of the immigration issue in U.S. civil society and politics.

## To Become Incarnate in the U.S.

We continue to be challenged by an over-appreciation of the American project, as I mentioned above. Perhaps this is the strongest ideology shaping how we "see" in the rubric "see-judge-act," the ideology with which those of us seeking to teach and witness to Francis' incarnational style must struggle and place in proper critical perspective.

In my own experience, becoming incarnate in that very divisive rhetoric of how best to fulfill the American project through supposedly Christian values has been my biggest challenge. Proposing that we read the American project from the hermeneutic of the preferential option for the poor means reading history from the lens of those who suffer from our own inability to humbly listen to each other and seek transformative unity with those with a diametrically opposite reading of how to be Christian in our society, both poor and privileged. It means bringing to the table a hermeneutic of humility, not of doctrinal accuracy or catechetical rigor. For those for whom the latter is a source of identity and strength amid a pluri-religious and seemingly threatening environment, practices that begin from the narrative of the suffering of the poor—without moral judgment, such as the U.S. bishops' mass at the border, will seem inappropriate and counter to the American project. Francis' incarnational style inspires me to stand at the very ideological fissures holding back Christians in the U.S. from engaging their particular contexts in incarnational praxis of love for others. Francis' incarnational witness has emboldened me to attend the call to collaboratively develop models that can break through ideological divides for Christians to unite for transformational acts of love.

MT Dávila is assistant professor of Christian ethics at Andover Newton Theological School. Her current efforts focus on the intersection of discipleship and public witness and activism among leaders of communities of faith. She has published in the areas of just war theory, racism and immigration, Christian ethics in the public square, and the use of the social sciences for Christian ethics. As a Roman Catholic laywoman, MT and her family (4 children and husband Rob) belong to St. Joseph's Parish in Malden, Massachusetts.

# A Fitting Home for Catholics

## Catholicism and the American Context

The Catholic Church is the Mystical Body of Christ, sent by her Lord to preach the Gospel to the entire world. But despite this universal mission, the Church faces very different situations in different countries and continents, for Catholic life has never been led in a vacuum. Even in her earliest days the fact that the Church emerged from a Jewish milieu meant the presence of certain cultural factors that accompanied the preaching of the Gospel. Similarly today in every country the Church is in the midst of a historical situation, favorable or not, which impacts upon her work. The Church very much exists in the world, and she cannot preach the Gospel without taking account of these varying historical circumstances in which she is placed. The task for Catholics will differ, for example, depending on whether the Church is hoping to recover a cultural role she once possessed or, as in this country, to find a way both to exist and to evangelize within a culture that has always been to one degree or another alien. Therefore my remarks apply pretty much exclusively to Catholic life in the United States. How that life will unfold in the coming years and decades of course no one knows, but based on a diagnosis of the present, one may offer, if not a prediction, then at least a hope or a wish of what the future might be.

Catholic life in the United States was shaped by the mass immigration that began in the middle of the 19th century, at first from Ireland and Germany, later from Italy, Poland and other eastern European nations. Because of this rapid influx of new members, the Church, as part of her pastoral care, was forced to focus on the question of the immigrants' adaptation to American life, a life that especially for rural immigrants must have been very different from their life in Europe. In the late 19th century this question of assimilation or Americanization was a major issue in the Church, and both clerical and lay Catholics debated, sometimes fiercely, the role that foreign-language parishes, or even dioceses, should play in the life of the Church in this country. But after the end of mass immigration in the 1920s these debates gradually died down. Today the question of Catholic assimilation into American life no longer seems like much of a live issue, but in fact it forms the background for the present situation of American Catholics. Beginning at least two generations ago Catholics began to feel fully at home in the United States, and there were fewer and fewer voices who questioned whether we really belonged here or could be true Americans. But this seemingly happy rapprochement came about only because Catholics increasingly lost whatever unique cultural identity we once had and conformed to the American cultural tradition rooted in Protestantism and 18th-century deism. The degree to which American culture was alien to Catholic ways of thinking and living was rarely faced in the triumphal march of American Catholics toward full acceptance by their fellow countrymen. Those who had originally raised uncomfortable questions, mostly German-American Catholics, were ignored and marginalized and ultimately forgotten by Catholics bent upon full acceptance as true Americans, regardless of the cost.

In the present historical situation of the United States almost all people, not excluding Catholics, identify, with varying degrees of awareness, with one or the other of our two large cultural-political blocs. That is, with either liberals or conservatives, the left or the right. I say *cultural-political,* not simply *political,* since the divide between these blocs extends far beyond politics, and includes even matters such as choice of food or dress or type of car driven. Unfortunately, neither of these blocs offers a fitting home for a Catholic. Both are fundamentally secular, indeed, part of the centuries-old revolt against Catholic faith and morals that began in earnest with the rise of Protestantism in the 16th century. The fundamental issue that American Catholics face today is to disengage themselves from their identification as either conservatives or liberals, and try to forge a cultural identity based on Catholic faith and tradition.

## Calvinism, Conservatism, and Catholic Social Thought

The tone of the American Church is being increasingly set by conservative Catholics. They rightly criticize those Catholics who support abortion or legalization of same-sex unions, and point out that such positions are in conflict with the Church's teaching. But most of these critics do not perceive that exactly the same kind of criticism can be made of conservative Catholics, who frequently dissent in significant ways from the Church's social doctrine or her teaching on war and peace. Moreover, most conservative Catholics seem to think that if only there were laws against certain of the most egregious evils, such as abortion, all would be well in society. Their vision of the Faith appears to be mostly a negative one; certain evils should be prohibited, but otherwise nothing much need be done at the level of society. The notion that the Catholic faith is meant to entirely transform a social order, to create a culture that values beauty and community above moneymaking and individualism, is foreign to them. In fact, both liberals and conservatives are more united than they realize, in that both in different ways accept the Lockean idea that society exists to further the pursuit of purely individual and this-worldly goals, and that the political community has no place in cultivating virtue and pointing us toward eternal life. Individualism has so colored our thinking that it is hard even to understand the role that the community should play in our lives, that we are all involved with each other and responsible for each other, and that we must consider our own welfare as necessarily linked with the welfare of the community. Indeed, Cardinal George of Chicago stated this at the Synod of Bishops for the Americas in November of 1997 when he said that U.S. citizens "are culturally Calvinist, even those who profess the Catholic faith," that American society "is the civil counterpart of a faith based on private interpretation of Scripture and private experience of God," and he contrasted this understanding of society

125

with one based on the Catholic Church's teaching of community and a vision of life greater than the individual.

If this is correct, the task for Catholics in the United States is to cultivate a sense of Catholic identity, an identity that goes beyond mere adherence to Catholic teaching on faith and morals—essential as that is—and recognizes that Catholic principles must permeate and change our entire social order. In fact, our task is to create, or perhaps in some degree to recreate, a Catholic culture or subculture. If this were seriously attempted, it would probably prove deeply troubling to most American Catholics, in that some of our most cherished cultural notions would have to be abandoned. The pursuit of individual happiness as the *summum bonum* of life, the measure of all things by their money value, excessive emphasis on rights—all these are matters that will be looked at in a different light by a Catholic culture.

## Culture or Compromise?

Too often appeals to revitalize Catholic life in America—most recently George Weigel's "Evangelical Catholicism"—for all its talk about proclaiming "Jesus Christ as the answer to the question that is every human life"—are in reality attempts to shore up the American polity, a polity based on 18th-century deism and which deliberately and explicitly excludes serious consideration of religious truth from public life. Weigel is fundamentally interested in what he thinks is "the true character of America and the nature of freedom," and he welcomes "those allies in the Evangelical Protestant, Mormon and traditional Jewish worlds who ... still hold to [John Courtney] Murray's four foundational truths of American democracy." Weigel states that the challenge is "to give America a new birth of freedom," and it's a bit hard to see what such a political project, or such curious religious allies, has to do with a proclamation of the Catholic faith.

In the late 19th century, in order to escape Protestant charges that we could not be good Americans, Catholics foisted upon themselves a notion of patriotism that pretty much involved an uncritical acceptance of the American project. There were only a few voices that objected, for most Catholics did not see that we could never approve of anything that called itself the *novus ordo seclorum,* as the Great Seal of the United

States puts it, for that phrase rightly applies only to the Church of God, not to any mere political order. We must be patriotic, certainly, but patriotic on our terms and in a Catholic sense. The best thing we could do for our country would be to offer it the authentic Gospel of Jesus Christ, along with an intellectual and cultural tradition of more substance and depth than that inherited from the Enlightenment.

Will something of this sort occur? Will a significant number of Catholics realize that both of the blocs into which American culture is divided are betrayals of Catholic faith and tradition? That obviously is difficult to say and probably futile to speculate. All one can do is again and again to remind Catholics of our duty and responsibility not only to adhere to the teaching of the Church on faith and morals, but to look to Catholic tradition as the fundamental locus of our thinking. This must not be understood as a call to cleave to a past understood merely as a set of rigid conventions or familiar practices. Rather it is an invitation to explore the rich world of Catholic tradition, to appropriate it and to offer what is true and good in it to ourselves and to our contemporaries. It is a past that embodies two millennia of reflection upon the saving truths of Christ's death and resurrection and their application to the human condition. Above all it is a catholic past, in as much as the Faith was given to all mankind and offers not only sacramental gifts of grace but whatever will make life more authentically human. To explore and appropriate this should be an exciting project for any Catholic, to transcend the dreary and ugly culture of materialism and contemplate a new vision both for the social order and for our individual lives. For in fact the question confronting Catholics is not over whether to adopt one set of opinions or another. It is over which culture we will dwell in, after what pattern we will order our thinking, and, as much as possible, our entire lives. Most American Catholics have unwittingly stumbled into one or another culture of secularism, of individualism, of a purely this-worldly concern. If we wish, we can alter that, but only if we are convinced that this is part of our vocation as Catholics. We all necessarily live within some culture. As Catholics, we cannot rightly do less than seek to dwell in a Catholic culture, our only fitting home on this earth.

 Thomas Storck has written widely on questions of Catholic culture and social doctrine. His last book was *Christendom and the West: Essays on Culture, Society and History,* available from the American Chesterton Society.

# American and Catholic in the Age of Francis: An Interview with Patrick Deneen

*Let's begin with a recent and much-noticed quote from Professor Robert George, who said, "The age of comfortable Catholicism is at an end." Any thoughts on this?*[1]

I read Robbie George's talk at the National Catholic Prayer Breakfast, which I found moving but also, in a sense, puzzling. It left me wondering exactly what that age of comfortable Catholicism was exactly—and when that was, what it looked like.

He acknowledges in his talk that there were times of outright and very difficult persecution of Catholics in this country. The kind of persecution that we're undergoing right now—in terms of aggressive governmental forms such as the HHS mandate and the advancing gay rights/gay marriage agenda—by comparison with the forms of persecution that existed in the 19th century are quite different and much paler. Which doesn't mean they're not to be taken seriously. But there were once pitched battles that took place, and corporal punish-

---

1  Elias Crim interviewed Prof. Deneen for Solidarity Hall in May of 2014.

ment, outright forms of discrimination against Catholics. Signs in windows reading "Blacks and Irish need not apply."

But it's clear that we're entering a time when we can say that there's a new, maybe more legalistic form of persecution, embedded in the legal system. But I think the heyday of Catholicism to which George was pointing, the time in which it looked as though the absence of any kind of persecution and the acceptance of Catholicism probably goes back to that period roughly between the 1950s into the 1990s. I think of Will Herberg's Protestant Catholic Jew which popularized the term "Judeo-Christian tradition," and of Robert Bellah's attempt to describe and to justify a form of American civil religion that can incorporate all the major faiths of the West. So maybe he's suggesting that this was a time when Catholics could feel at home in America.

But I find myself a bit puzzled and even a bit skeptical about that claim because the terms on which the broader culture offered its acceptance of Catholicism included a demand that it act in some ways a lot more Protestant. That it increasingly privatize its claims.

Think back to the suspicions about John F. Kennedy preceding the election of 1960. The demand that he appear before the Baptist ministers convention in Houston in order to explain how it is that he would not govern as a Catholic. Kennedy responded by stating that his Catholicism would not enter into the picture and, if an occasion ever arose leading him to choose between his oath to the Constitution and his Catholic conscience, he would resign his office.

Some thirty years later, in a speech given here at Notre Dame, Governor Mario Cuomo in some ways again broached this question, now in relation to a post-Roe v. Wade world in which the dominant question was, would Catholic politicians seek to advance a pro-life view. And Mario Cuomo famously stated, going a step further than JFK, that while he himself was personally pro-life, in his approach to governance he had to follow the law of the land. Thus his Catholicism could be taken as a private faith that had no bearing on the public world.

So we could say that this was a period in which there was a growing acceptance of Catholics but the terms of that acceptance demanded that Catholicism be acceptable in the eyes of a predominantly Protestant culture. Catholicism was acceptable to the extent that it could be regarded as a private faith, without its core tenets being brought to bear on matters in the public square.

If we think further about these terms of acceptance, we could say that the contemporary crisis of Catholicism is due to that settlement in which Catholics agreed to a Protestant understanding of their faith. And as a result, Catholicism has increasingly waned as an influence in the lives of Catholics. To the point that we have either a nominal form of Catholicism in America or among the young, an extraordinary dropping-off from the faith.

So this time which Robbie George may be recalling with some nostalgia seems to me to have laid down some of the conditions for the result he is now descrying. So I would simply respond by saying I don't think there has ever been a time of comfortable Catholicism in America. It's always been seen as a place apart: Catholics had their own schools, hospitals, their own set of norms. That period of time is captured quite wonderfully by Alan Ehrenhalt, in his wonderful book about Chicago's old neighborhoods, The Lost City.

But that was also the time in which suspicion of Catholics ran pretty high, precisely because they were seen as a culture apart. So acceptance had to be on terms that left that "ghetto culture" behind for the norms of a culturally Protestant society. To the point where today I think many Catholics are culturally Protestant.

*As Cardinal George has pointed out before.*

Right. And as I see every day in my students, most of whom fit this description of nominally Catholic, culturally Protestant.

*Which they must be surprised to learn, surely.*

(Laughs.) I'm not sure they ever learn it!

*You've written about the influence of John Courtney Murray on American Catholicism and the debate around his influence. How would you characterize that debate?*

Murray understood that if the American founding was understood as essentially liberal and grounded in the Enlightenment, that understanding would make America in hospitable to Catholicism and its understanding of the human person. As well as Catholicism's traditional teaching that human society exists to orient people toward the good. Which then leads to an appeal to the common good, as opposed to some utilitarian calculus or aggregation of preferences.

Murray, knowing all this, made it his project to articulate a view of the founding as not owing to the liberalism of Enlightenment philosophy but to something in fact unbeknownst to those very founding figures. He argues that their work rested on and appealed to a public philosophy which could be traced back to antiquity, through Aristotelian and Thomistic traditions.

*A natural law tradition, that is.*

Exactly. If you read We Hold These Truths, the heart of his argument is in his phrase, The Founders built better than they knew. He's saying that in a way which they might unaware of, they were using materials foreign to them and which, had the Founders reflected on these ideas, they would have rejected. Yet these older materials formed a kind of sub-basement beneath the Founders' notions taken from Locke or even Thomas Hobbes. These social contractarian ideas are in deep contradiction to the understanding of Aristotle, as articulated by Aquinas, that man is by nature a social, political animal. As opposed to the Enlightenment notion that human beings are by nature autonomous, independent, rights-bearing creatures without a corresponding set of duties.

Murray understood that if this latter view of the founding were correct, then Catholicism would be incompatible with America. Drawing on earlier figures such as Orestes Brownson, the great Catholic convert of the 19th century, he suggested there was this kind of deeper substructure to American society grounded in this older tradition. He went even further to suggest that in this understanding, America could even be seen as more Catholic than Protestant, adding that those Catholics who had arrived in the 19th century could help perfect America through a new national self-understanding.

*Which sounds like just the thesis Murray's more recent Catholic interpreters and champions were arguing.*

Absolutely. The individuals around the founding of the journal First Things—Father Richard John Neuhaus, George Weigel, Michael Novak and others who embraced Murray's view. The debate within the more tradition-minded Catholic world is thus about whether or not Murray got the Founding right—not over the question of whether Catholicism is compatible with Lockean liberalism. Pretty much all sides agree that it is not. The debate is whether or not the founders did indeed build better than they knew.

Figures like David Schindler, Alasdair MacIntyre and others have argued that Murray's understanding is flawed, a product of a kind of wishful thinking, and that American was in fact founded amidst the philosophical currents of Enlightenment optimism. They would claim that Catholicism has always been a kind of foreign entity within the American settlement, within which Catholics have inserted themselves in order to make a home. And thus the need for the fatal compromises with the dominant understanding of the human, as we spoke of earlier here.

*The recent dustup around this subject—and in a way the spur to create this anthology—was a piece you published this February in the American Conservative called "A Catholic Showdown Worth Watching." The charge arouse that to hold views such as you just described was to be "illiberal," in John Zmirak's term—a curious choice of words.*

Certainly I never used that word in my piece nor would I. And I was genuinely surprised at the response to that piece. It received by far the most visits of any piece I've ever published online, currently standing at about 100,000 hits. Oddly enough—and I don't mean to sound naïve here—but I meant that piece to be largely informational, not contentious.

At the time I was preparing a response to a recent book by David Schindler as my part of a roundtable being held at the John Paul II Institute. So I was thinking about Schindler and his debates with Murray, Weigel, Novak and so on. So I thought of trying to inform the wider public of this ongoing debate that many people were unaware of. None of what I wrote, by the way, was new.

My conclusion is that the piece set off a kind of firestorm, largely because of the changed relationship between America and Catholicism today. I think many people have been inchoately thinking about these things with a wide sense of unease. So that among orthodox Catholics there's the sense that the project of the last fifty years—to make Catholicism at home in America—may not have worked.

And their realization that the problem may not lie with a particular set of electoral or partisan arrangements but more deeply, in the DNA of America and of Catholicism. So the piece's riveting effect had to do with its timing and what's going on currently in the Church and more broadly in the culture and politics.

I'm deeply unhappy with the characterization of those reflecting on the potential tension if not hostility between liberalism and Catholicism as somehow illiberal. Moreover, I think that this debate, such that it is, is not between liberalism and illiberalism—or even anti-liberalism. It is a debate between two different conceptions of liberty.

Starting with the dominant American understanding: if I ask my students, what is liberty or what is freedom, the answer I get 98% of the time—here at Notre Dame—is that liberty is being able to do what I want to do. And that is the definition according to Hobbes or to Locke. Liberty is the absence of an obstacle to the fulfillment of my desires.

By the Catholic, Christian and classical understanding, liberty is the freedom to do that which is good or right. Therefore liberty depends upon a deep understanding of self-rule and the governance of our wills, desires and passions.

So I would say that I'm actually a proponent of liberty, liberty as properly understood. To use a phrase like illiberal is deeply unhelpful: it seeks to obfuscate the fact that there is a deep disagreement between the liberal understanding of liberty and the Catholic or classical understanding. And I would argue that the latter is the true understanding and thus it is more truly liberal, if we know that word's connection with liberty.

So rather than accepting the erroneous term "illiberal" Catholics, those who share our views might consider not the adjective "radical"—

which sounds vaguely revolutionary or anarchic—but the adverb "radically" which suggests going back to one's roots.

Consider the way in which the career of Catholicism in this country went from being persecution to seeming acceptance and now back to persecution again. There are some who pine for that period of seeming acceptance and would like it to be the norm to which we appeal.

I think the idea of being radically Catholic at least forces us to entertain the possibility that Catholicism, when connected to its roots, will always stand in a critical position toward a predominantly liberal culture and politics. This means it must be critical not only of those we consider liberals by contemporary political labels—i.e., those on the left—but it must also engage in a much more radically critical way with those on the political right today. Within the current American political context, both those on the left and the right are most fundamentally liberal.

So part of the reaction to the American Conservative piece had to do with the 40- or 50-year understanding on the part of orthodox or traditionalist Catholics that our hopes could be vested in the Republican Party. The response had less to do with any criticism of Catholicism per se but was much more about the betrayal of partisan allegiances.

*And during these same decades there is also the impact of U.S. foreign policy and the fate of the U.S. economy.*

Possibly the figure with the most critical commentary on this alignment between our foreign policy and our economics has been Andrew Bacevich. His series of books and essays has powerfully argued that our aggressive and imperial foreign policy has worked hand in glove with an increasingly deracinated, globalized and impersonal economic forces.

It's interesting—we're speaking the day after Memorial Day. If you think about it, our allegiance to place and people has in some ways been put in the service of a set of movements which deracinate, displace and denationalize our economic lives. It's almost politically incorrect to juxtapose these two forces but I think Bacevich, among others, has documented how these noble, self-sacrificial actions and appeals have been used toward very paradoxical ends.

On the one hand, these forces have worked to undermine those very virtues while also benefitting those placeless elites who act from an absence of any devotion to particular people and particular places in favor of a globalized economic system.

*Could we say that as opposed to the liberal faith in systems and in the ability of the social sciences to lend some predictability to large social projects, a Catholic anthropology sees things differently?*

Yes, and it's interesting to note that our current politics asks us, to which impersonal force will you swear allegiance? If you're on the political left, your allegiance should lie with an increasingly distant and impersonal state. As was declared—repeatedly—at the last Democratic National Convention, the state "is the only thing that we all belong to." This is exactly what Thomas Hobbes was getting at. For us as individuals, all other allegiances are rendered private except for that to the state. The DNC's statement is the culmination of a project going back 500 years.

At the same time, those on the political right in America declare their allegiance to the impersonal forces of the market. Which is not the purportedly benign hand of a distant government but the invisible hand of several billion individual choosers.

So it's precisely here that Catholic anthropology rejects both these forces—not because they're viewed as illegitimate agents in our world. After all, Catholic social teaching regard both the state and the market as legitimate and necessary actors for a flourishing human life. But CST argues that neither should be dominant and both should be ordered properly in order that families, communities and regions—and ultimately the world itself—can flourish.

So Catholic teachings would maintain that those groupings closest to us personally keep in sight our solidarity with the rest of the human community and that indeed solidarity is best expressed in terms of this kind of subsidiarity. You might say that subsidiarity works most effectively on behalf of human beings the closer it is them personally, until they lack the capacity to solve a problem at a more local level. At that point we may need to look to more distant solutions. This is not an argument for mere local prejudice or parochialism. It's the insight that human beings are best motivated and will assume the most responsibility when they act on issues close at hand.

*And now, coming down to our views of the local, please contrast for us your sense of your previous life in D.C. (at Georgetown U.) with life in South Bend.*

In one way, life in D.C. is like life in any major urban area in the country. It's filled with lots of opportunities—cultural, artistic, gustatory, etc. But it also resembles other urban areas in being more transitory, somewhat more anonymous, although one can fight against that. D.C. is attractive to that portion of our population that values cosmopolitanism, a non-judgmental toleration and diversity (sometimes understood by another measure as indifference), a high level of secularity, a much greater adherence to mobility, lower birth rates, etc. The kinds of things Charles Murray has described in his book Coming Apart.

Add to all that the fact that D.C. is the imperial center. It's fascinating to know that some seven of the wealthiest counties in the U.S. are in the greater D.C. area. If you reflect on what exactly it is that this region makes or produces, you may be led to conclude that this one economic fact shows we're at the end of our imperial tether. When so much of the nation's wealth is aggregating here in order to create political influence, you'd be tempted to say the game's up.

It's deeply disconcerting to me that not only do you have so many liberals there who would declare that the only thing we have in common is that we all belong to the state, but innumerable contemporary conservatives are drawn to D.C. and spend their entire lives in this area. The latter were the people who put me most at unease when I lived there. Because they seemed to have concluded that the only way to decrease the influence of D.C. is by taking it over and running it. Which eventually means you become co-opted into and even invested in the course of the empire.

South Bend is obviously a very different place—a kind of down in the mouth Rustbelt city that's slowly coming back which has a consciousness that it must work hard to make itself again an attractive place. We have a very young new mayor, Pete Buttigieg, whom I've met and spoken with. He's a Harvard grad, recipient of a Rhodes Scholarship, and then worked for a big consulting firm in D.C. before coming back to his hometown to run for mayor. At this moment, moreover, he's serving a six-month tour of duty in Afghanistan.

He's the kind of person that South Bend has unfortunately lost over the years in big numbers as they moved off to places like D.C. So the first big difference between the two cities is that people who want to bring back a place like South Bend are also making a conscious decision not to live in a place like D.C. They want to be in a place where they and their families can feel rooted in a community which is there not because of all its attractions but because it offers an ongoing and thick set of relationships with other people.

Add to that—and maybe it's not coincidental—that South Bend is the location of the nation's pre-eminent Catholic university. So the people who commit to being here for that reason also tend to be deeply committed Catholics, often with large families, involved in multiple ways with their parish life, the Catholic Worker house here in town, among other remarkable Catholic networks here.

So it is exactly in places like this that those people deeply committed to the Church and to living their faith ought to begin thinking about how to change the culture. Not by moving to Washington D.C. and trying to take over the imperial administration—which will only corrupt you, inevitably and inexorably.

Rather, to rebuild all these places abandoned by the upwardly mobile and elite there's a desperate need for people committed to family and to neighborhood. That's the big difference to me about coming here—to be part of that kind of community.

*On Mayor Pete's team, I wonder if you've met Scott Ford, the executive director of community investment. He's a former student of our mutual friend, Phil Bess [professor of architecture at Notre Dame and author of* Till We Have Built Jerusalem*].*

I have not met Scott yet, but it's clear to me that Philip has had influence here. I don't know if you're familiar with the plans for the reconfiguration of the downtown streets with a view toward restoring a mixed-use, walkable downtown. And the downtown has lots of potential—the river, especially.

There was a terrible decision made some years ago to make four-lane one-way roads running through the center of the city, turning it into a kind of giant north-south thoroughfare. But now that may be corrected by turning those into two-way streets and reduced to three lane boulevards. That should send the traffic seeking other routes outside the city so that people will become again desirous of walking around the downtown area.

So as Catholic thinkers like Phil Bess have shown, it's taken us fifty years for this experiment in centering human habitation around the automobile to finally demonstrate that it's not beneficial for human flourishing.

In fact, I'm working on a book now in which I note that in some respects America itself has been the proving ground for the dominant philosophies of the Western tradition. The philosophies that you could broadly associate with Christendom, with origins in antiquity and most strongly associated with Catholicism, is one that arrived from elsewhere on these shores. Another is early modern liberalism of the Hobbesian-Lockean cast which becomes, as Murray recognized, the official philosophy of America.

And another still, developed in the nineteenth century, is the philosophy which regards us as historically constituted creatures that progress through history and which we label as progressivism. So what I'm suggesting is that these three are the dominant political philosophies developed in the West. And that all arrived more or less intact in America so that much of American history has to do with the ways in which these three strains of thought have interacted. I consider how often two of them have combined in opposition to the third, then becoming instantiated as part of our public policy.

So my primary conclusions are to note that indeed ideas do have consequences and that America has become the main battleground for these three ways of thinking about how we should live our lives. My broader conclusion is that much of our contemporary debate has been between progressivism and early modern liberalism—sometimes misleading labeled conservatism. And America has been very successful at ensuring that the first of these traditions—the ancient Christian tradition—is divided into one of these two camps. The irony here is that adherents of the Christian tradition have had to conform themselves to one of the two dominant modern philosophies, with the result that the powerful witness of that ancient tradition has been hamstrung and compromised by this division.

*This compromise leads me to ask: Probably most of the contributors to this anthology feel they are not merely or solely pro-life but rather whole-life. And that the next wave of evangelization needs to be more about social justice than about any of the other hot-button, mailing-list issues that have preoccupied American Catholics in recent years.*

I like the phrase "whole-life." And it gets us back to the way in which partisan alignments reflect, as I was just suggesting, deeper philosophical demands. And how the latter have erroneously compromised the ability of many Catholics to more fully articulate precisely what John Paul II called a culture of life. The hallmark of such a culture can't simply be a demand for a certain decision by the Supreme Court. Or that we have to win certain kinds of elections in order to ensure certain kinds of judicial decisions. Or even that we can reduce a culture of life to a certain set of legal prescriptions.

Not that these are not important. But to put the dominant emphasis in this legal sphere would suggest that a series of fatal compromises have been made, compromises that thwart our ability to think fully about what a culture of life could mean—for a whole life.

So in this way if we allow Catholic social teachings—both on life issues and on all the other key issues as well—to be divided from the rest of our concerns for reasons of political expediency, then we've already fatally compromised our ability to think about a culture of life.

It seems to me that the deepest undercurrents that inform contemporary understandings of the human being defines our selves as autonomous actors, self-owning and self-possessing bodies, shaped not only by a culture dominated by a kind of libertine set of sexual ethics but deeply shaped by a set of economic understandings that also regards us as a set of libertine self-possessing actors. There's a deep continuity between what we often divide politically as libertinism on the left with regard to sexual matters and libertinism on the right with regard to economic matters. And our contemporary political alignment would tell us that these two things have nothing to do with each other.

So a theory of whole life would necessarily have to see not only a reconsideration of the entire legal approach to understanding life issues but would have to understand this in continuity with a set of economic and social forces. Just as much as the legal domain, these latter forces influence the way we see ourselves as self-owning, autonomous creatures.

*We might note that the economics profession is in need, some would say, of a kind of Copernican revolution, partly because it is currently undergoing a theoretical crisis.*

It seems to me to be striking, and overwhelmingly the case, that we are reaching a kind of crisis in all these areas more or less simultaneously, because they have all been informed by a deeply mistaken notion of the human person. And this mistake has taken roughly 200 years to work itself out. So one of the problems of liberal society, we could say, is that it tends to treat all of these various issues and crises as separable.

After all, one of the operating assumptions of liberalism is that you put every object, every set of issues into individual and isolated boxes. We treat subjects in the same way we treat human beings—each is autonomous. So these crises in these several realms—economic, political, social, familial—are not coincidental. A more Catholic understanding would see the deep interconnections between all these facets of life.

I agree there's a crisis in economics, although I don't know that many economists recognize it as such—certainly some do. And if not in economics, we certainly have a crisis in our economy, one connected to similar crises in these other areas.

*So then what do you expect Pope Francis' influence will be in these matters?*

Pope Francis has certainly become a real touchstone of debate in the American context. And I think that has a lot to do with Francis as a person. But it also has a lot to do with a concatenation of recent events that Francis helps to bring into focus, although they would have come into focus regardless. You could say providentially and otherwise, Francis is the right person in the right place at the right time. I think that's the case.

But a couple of things we already knew to be true before Francis' election as pope. The American Church is in crisis. The Church is moving south, in terms of its adherents. Western societies, as Benedict understood very well, are becoming increasingly and overtly hostile to the Church. Francis in a way brings into focus several of these trends which were already underway. He becomes a flashpoint for these trends because of who he is and because he brings into focus many of these developments in the modern world.

I don't know how long Francis' papacy will be—he's getting on in years—but I think he has begun a shift in the Church's relationship with modernity which had offered a kind of hope for a time that it could find a modus vivendi with Catholicism. So I think Francis may be our first post-modern pope—not in the Derridean or Foucauldian sense. Nor is he a pope in the nineteenth century style of wanting to hold back modernity. Nor is he a twentieth-century pope saying that we can find a way to get along with, cooperate with modernity.

I think he's saying the Church has to move beyond modernity, simply by living a more Christ-like witness in the world—not seeking to make accommodations with the dominant regimes, even liberalism. Obviously the Church has to operate in the world and it will have to reflect on how to do that. But its dominant commitment has to be to the Gospel and to evangelizing the good news and to living in a Christ-like manner.

And for all the politicized commentary about Francis you get in the media, both on the right and on the left, the fact that he has struck such a deep chord with so many people reflects, I think, a yearning for something deeper than the terribly superficial, deeply dissatisfying, materialist, flattened and unhopeful horizon that modernity has offered to humanity. So he's pointing toward something beyond the Church's two reactions to modernity thus far, in the nineteenth and then in the twentieth centuries.

*Any thoughts on the particular sequence of recent popes: John Paul to Benedict to Francis?*

It's extraordinary—an extraordinary sequence of popes.

*What have we done do deserve these guys—we great laypeople? (Laughter.) What have we done?*

Yes, exactly. Each of them in his own way the right man at the right time—and articulating in just the right way how the Church had to exist in the modern world. And the American tendency to divide these papacies, so that you can be pro-Benedict or anti-Francis or the reverse, is again a deep sign of a pathology that a radically Catholic commitment hopes to correct.

That our deepest hope and joy ought to lie in understanding the deeper continuities among all three of these papacies. In some ways, I think these papacies embody the spiritual virtues of faith, hope and love: John Paul, the great articulator of the faith (and its relationship to reason), then Benedict, among whose great achievements was giving a new hope to the modern world. And can Francis be described as anything other than caritas, love in action.

And yet that falsely divides them who were themselves the embodiment of all three of these virtues. But the Church has always understood that different times call for different expressions of the faith.

Patrick Deneen holds a Ph.D. from from Rutgers University. He is professor of political science at Notre Dame University. His published writings include *The Odyssey of Political Theory* and *Democratic Faith*.

# The Blind Leading Himself: From Incoherence to Pope Francis

## A Winding Path and Political Homelessness

I hope that the reader will be indulgent with the one now addressing you, who has the introspective faculties of a rear axle. The closest I usually come is when I laugh at myself in the mirror as I examine what time and destiny have worked on my overall appearance. But I do have a private mythology about myself that will not allow me to shrink from my duty here to inflict on you a more or less subjective assessment of the experience of being Catholic in the time of Pope Francis.

To set the matter in context I must point out that I spent most of my young and middle adulthood as a political agnostic. As counterintuitive as it may seem, my working life as an attorney seemed to demand it. Sometimes I stumble into attracting attention, and I couldn't afford having prospective jurors secretly hating me for my socio-political opinions. Besides, although there are notable exceptions, spending any time around politicians in general will cure one of anticipating the arrival of Utopia from that sector. The desire for power is a soul twisting characteristic, even worse than practicing law.

The cure for this disease began to be applied when George W. Bush and Co. decided to march into Iraq for no good reason at all. When operations began I decided to let my feelings be known by going around and referring to "our invasion of Poland—I mean, Iraq." The invasion brought home to me an important theological truth. As it began to look as though the U.S. was really going to go through with it, I begged the Almighty not to let our national leadership do something so palpably stupid. The answer my prayer received is a matter of public record. As it turns out, God doesn't take away anyone's free will, even in response to fervent prayer.

I also received some enlightenment in the area of intra-Church disputation at this time. As you are doubtlessly aware, there is a considerable but diminishing breed of Catholic who believes that the Church should give up her old fuddy-duddy ways regarding such issues as birth control and the slaying of unborn infants (euphemistically referred to as "abortion"). Now I had been in the cheering section of those who wrote and spoke to the effect that Catholicism should remain Catholic, being little impressed with the suggestion that the Church should be blown about by the winds of the *zeitgeist*. So much a partisan did I become that I subscribed to a well-known periodical that positioned itself in favor of traditional Church teaching.

But then the invasion of Iraq happened. I've already made it clear that I was against it, but, more importantly, Pope John Paul II was against it, and there was good reason for that: invading a country that hasn't attacked you is a clear violation of the Just War Doctrine, which I remembered having read about in the Catechism. Alas, the aforementioned periodical came out in favor of the invasion. Indeed, it even went so far as to suggest that the Just War Doctrine should be revisited. So it was a bad thing when Catholic "liberals" said that the Church's teaching on birth control should be revised, but it was okay when Catholic "conservatives" called the Just War Doctrine into question. I began to feel as though I had subscribed, not to a Catholic magazine, but to a Republican one, and a neoconservative Republican one at that. As a card carrying non-partisan for the vast majority of my adult life, I took offense. I wasn't offended because they were Republican neo-cons; I was offended because they presented themselves as by-the-book Catholics, but capitulated to the Republican Party line as soon it came into conflict with their religion. I didn't renew my subscription.

## Out of the Silence and Onto the Airwaves

The Iraq War radicalized me, and so when the opportunity came to produce and host a show on a local progressive talk radio station, KRXA 540 AM in Monterey, I took it. The way it came about was that a good friend of mine had a show on KRXA and asked me if I would be willing to guest host one day. It was an interesting request, since I was sure I had never voiced any strong political views to him, and there was no way for him to know that I wouldn't show up and advocate the return of the Confederacy. Seeing that it would be a new experience, and that it wouldn't involve breaking the law, I assented.

I caught the bug immediately. I started calling in to my friend's show, and, after I had voiced my opinions a few times on-air, I asked the station owner, Hal Ginsberg, if I could produce a show at KRXA. He put his head right in the noose and agreed. I arranged for advertisers, and went on the air every Thursday night. Over time others joined the show as co-hosts. They were Billy Sunshine, Mark Leonard, and Tony Rudy, and all of those were fake names. I used a fake name too: Jack Hart. The reason for using fake names was not because we were embarrassed, but because some listeners might otherwise track you down to your residence, and these are rarely from the sanest sampling. Now I was thrilled to be doing this, but I faced two initial challenges.

The first was that a talk show on politics is supposed to cover serious issues, but I am not a serious man. Indeed, I am a very ridiculous man. Sometimes I even got yelled at by judges for being a ridiculous man. So how was I going to be serious on the radio? As it turned out, I couldn't manage it at all. The show ended up being one where the hosts didn't take themselves seriously while discussing serious topics. It actually worked pretty well, and we ended up with regular listeners.

The second challenge was that I wasn't a political progressive. I'm still not. I was really concerned that the listener base might tar and feather me, since talk radio isn't for exchanging ideas so much as to affirm listeners in what they already believe. Conservatives listen to conservative radio, and liberals listen to liberal radio. But I had another moment of radicalization that afforded me some liberal credibility.

Seventeen-year-old Nataline Sarkisyan, a leukemia patient, was in need of a liver transplant according to her doctors. Cigna Corporation, her insurance company, disagreed. Her family fought a two week battle to get the insurance company to reverse its decision, and after protests and pleading from Nataline's doctors, the company finally reversed itself. But it was too late; Nataline died. Although it cannot be said with certainty that the procedure would have saved Nataline's life, it wasn't given a chance; Cigna Corporation didn't want to spend the money. And it must be pointed out that the procedure wasn't proposed by a cabal of witch doctors and astrologers. It was UCLA physicians who were urging Cigna to reverse its decision. From this I was convinced that the profit motive must be forever banished from medical decision making, and I became an advocate for universal, single-payer health coverage. I still am, no matter how many times I get called a socialist. At the conclusion of each show I would sign off with the words: "Remember Nataline Sarkisyan."

Still, I didn't move completely over into the progressive camp. I was still pro-life, and I declined to be secretive about it. I know for a fact that Hal got complaints about it, but to his credit he kept me on the air. His tolerance of diverse points of view is rare in the business, as I know from the fact that when I moved from California, and got on another liberal radio station, it wasn't long before I was shown the door precisely because of my pro-life position.

I did make the effort to convince my listeners that being pro-life is quite consistent with progressivism, and to that end I invited a representative of the Democrats for Life of America to come on the show two or three times. So impressed was I that I actually joined the Democrats largely to become a member of Democrats for Life. Here was a group that agreed that infants should not be slain, and, at the same time, that society has an obligation to care for the poor and needy. It was a group that made the observation that should be obvious: that a critical strategy in ending abortions is to do away with the social incentives to get them.

My membership in the group was never active, and was thwarted by two developments. The first was that the Republican Party started to subject pro-life Democrats to special targeting with a fair measure of success. This town ain't big enough for two pro-life parties, and the Republicans wanted to make sure that pro-life votes were also votes to cut food stamps. The result was that pro-life Democrats were even further marginalized within their party.

The second was when the Obama administration decided to force businesses to fund artificial birth control through employee health insurance, even abortifacient birth control, whether or not the business owners were conscientiously opposed to it. That is a regulation that affects Catholic business owners most of all, and, since I am a Catholic, I was furious. Of course, no one in power particularly cares if I'm furious, but I wasn't going to be a member of a political party that spits in my eye.

So I was partyless once again, and it looked as though I would stay that way indefinitely, since there wasn't a third party around that didn't support something that offended my conscience. I wished for a political party that embodied Catholic Social Teaching, and wishing was pretty much what I did to bring it about. I'm not the organizing type. Most of the time I have a hard time convincing myself to do anything. So I wished that somebody else would try to organize such a party. Somebody did.

## A New Environment and New Possiblities

When we moved from California, I also retired, and my wife of endless faith was looking forward to my being more useful around the house. She was not ignorant of the fact that my attempts to fix things usually results in my breaking them even more, but she was hoping that some hitherto unexcavated usefulness would emerge from my having more time on my hands. What I did instead was goof around endlessly on the internet. Now God loves fools and drunks, and although I gave up drinking more than 20 years ago, I can still avail myself of the former designation and stumble into good luck. The good luck I stumbled into this time came in the form of a young man by the name of David Frost, who was trying to develop an internet presence for the purpose of forming a Christian Democratic Party in the United States. Serious users of the internet will know David as a musician, archer, and aficionado of disturbing works of art.

I contacted David, and found that he was indeed trying to start a political party that would be based in Catholic Social Teaching. I told him that I would be thrilled to do whatever I could, although my competence in politics was limited to getting a bookstore employee to give me a discount on a damaged volume. David didn't concern himself with my protestations of ineptitude, since every good movement needs a cheering section, and he had already found organizational talent in one Kirk Morrison.

Still, I wanted to be useful on some level, so I gave some consideration to what I might be able to contribute. After some intense thinking on the matter that lasted almost twenty minutes, I gave David a call and suggested that we could have a webzine that would embody our thinking on political and social issues. We could call it "Christian Democracy," after Christian Democracy. I was excited about the idea, and at once fell into an ecstasy of grandiose delusion.

Of course, I needed writers; this couldn't just be my private blog. So I got Kirk Morrison to commit to a monthly article, and quickly found that, notwithstanding his predilection for bow ties, he has some very interesting and innovative ideas about how to make American society a saner and more humane place to live. I also got my old college buddy, Phil Ropp, to agree to a monthly contribution. I can listen for hours to Phil; he is brilliant and a first-rate writer. I like to stay on good terms with him, because he also knows enough about me to send me to the electric chair. The best way I can describe Phil is to ask you to imagine a combination of John the Baptist, Menno Simons, and Ernie Harwell.

Eventually it was deemed prudent to run *Christian Democracy* as separate from the party founded by David Frost. The webzine started with a definite and specific mission and point of reference, whereas the party was still deciding in democratic fashion what it would become. The members of the party are now calling themselves the Solidarity Party, and Kirk, its chairman, still makes monthly contributions to the webzine.

As time went on, more writers came on as monthly contributors. Father Mike Van Cleve of the Archdiocese of Galveston-Houston started sending us his monthly reflections. His down-to-earth but profound insights have added a dimension to Christian Democracy that I can't imagine being without. Doran Hunter and Amir Azarvan have come on board, and have provided us with the kind of first rate writing talent that I will put up against any publication. Moreover, there have been one time contributors that have greatly enhanced our credibility and quality; notable among these was Mark Shea, a prolific Catholic author, who writes for the *National Catholic Register*. After awhile I had to come to the conclusion that God was blessing our work, since even I don't have that much dumb luck.

About three months after we came online, Jorge Mario Bergoglio became Pope Francis. Now before Pope Francis came along, the bulk of Catholic Social Teaching could be found in papal encyclicals. This made it easy to put forward almost anything as in keeping with the social doctrine of the Church, since most people don't read encyclicals. One prominent politician even tried to suggest that his proposal to cut Social Security and Medicare was justified by Church teaching. Our humble effort to point out that Catholic Social Teaching demands such things as living wages, the right to organize labor unions, and the universal destination of goods, stood no human chance against the well organized and well financed project to make the Catholic Church a department of the Republican Party.

But Pope Francis has made the social doctrine of the Church widely known through his very public pronouncements. He has made it clear that the Church is decidedly on the side of the impoverished, that workers must be treated and paid fairly, and that justice in today's world will require the redistribution of wealth from the rich to the poor. Those who have declared otherwise have been justly rendered sheepish. I like to think that *Christian Democracy*, given the timing of its coming into existence, is a small part of the renewal of Catholic Social Teaching heralded by the Holy Father.

Jack Quirk is editor of the webzine Christian Democracy. He is a practicing Catholic who hopes that, with continuing practice, he may one day get good at it. Jack has been married to his wife, Linda, for 28 years. They have six children.

# Snippets from an Exhortation: The Anti-Modernism of Pope Francis

The narrative that has been played out since the election of Jorge Bergoglio is one of a Pope ready to overturn all the doctrines of the Church, ordain women priests, change the teaching on marriage and homosexuality, and generally turn the Catholic Church into a minor caucus within the Democratic Party. This narrative was advanced by the press spin on Francis' interview with *La Civiltà Cattolica*, or rather, on selected snippets from that interview.

The narrative has now moved on to the Pope's apostolic exhortation, *Evangelii Gaudium*. As with the infamous interview, the conversation has centered on snippets from the document. And there are two sets of snippets which have attracted the most comment: the sections on economics and the comments on traditionalism. The secular press has concentrated almost entirely on the former. Concerning the latter, the Pope's comments seemed gratuitous and have caused deep pain and sorrow among the Church's most ardent and faithful supporters.

I would like to suggest that when one moves beyond these snippets, a totally different picture emerges, one in which traditionalists can take heart and one which must drive liberals—and especially economic liberals—to despair. For when we look at the exhortation *in toto,* what emerges is an attack on the entire Enlightenment project: an attack on secularism, rationalism, relativism, individualism, economic liberalism, coupled with a defense of the family, popular piety, and Christian culture. And even in the attack on traditionalists, what is being questioned is not the commitment to the Tradition itself, but a certain form of traditional-*ism,* the conversion of the tradition into an ideology with a political agenda; it is a critique that Traditionalists would do well to take to heart in an act of self-examination. Overall, it is a document which Traditionalists should welcome; one which validates the concerns they have expressed since the beginning of the modern era. It is a document which refuses to accept the basic tenet of liberalism, the one that marginalizes the Church as an institution which should confine itself to the otherworldly and leave this world to the social scientist, the businessman, the politician, and the bureaucrat.

Allow me to read a few additional snippets, not with a view to giving an exhaustive analysis of the document, which would certainly exhaust the reader, but merely to suggest that there is more here than one meets in the popular press. And a good place to start is with the attack on secularism and rationalism, as in this snippet:

> The process of secularization tends to reduce the faith and the Church to the sphere of the private and personal. Furthermore, by completely rejecting the transcendent, it has produced a growing deterioration of ethics, a weakening of the sense of personal and collective sin, and a steady increase in relativism. These have led to a general sense of disorientation, especially in the periods of adolescence and young adulthood which are so vulnerable to change. As the bishops of the United States of America have rightly pointed out, while the Church insists on the existence of objective moral norms which are valid for everyone, "there are those in our culture who portray this teaching as unjust, that is, as opposed to basic human rights. Such claims usually follow from a form of moral relativism that is joined, not without

inconsistency, to a belief in the absolute rights of individuals. (64)

This section provides a target-rich environment, covering culture, secularism, transcendence, ethics, sin, absolute rights, and relativism. These topics form a motif that will run throughout the Exhortation, and are examined in some detail, especially in relation to their effects on culture, social order and, above all, evangelization.

Underneath these problems, for Francis, lies individualism and its associated moral subjectivism:

> We should recognize how in a culture where each person wants to be bearer of his or her own subjective truth, it becomes difficult for citizens to devise a common plan which transcends individual gain and personal ambitions. (61)

Connected to this secularism is the problem of a rationalism which excludes, *a priori,* any transcendence:

> At other times, contempt is shown for writings which reflect religious convictions, overlooking the fact that religious classics can prove meaningful in every age; they have an enduring power to open new horizons, to stimulate thought, to expand the mind and the heart. This contempt is due to the myopia of a certain rationalism. Is it reasonable and enlightened to dismiss certain writings simply because they arose in a context of religious belief? (256)

All of these ills result in a "cultural crisis" which has profound effects on marriage and the family:

> The family is experiencing a profound cultural crisis, as are all communities and social bonds. In the case of the family, the weakening of these bonds is particularly serious because the family is the fundamental cell of society, where we learn to live with others despite our differences and to belong to one another; it is also the place where parents pass on the faith to their children. Marriage now tends to be viewed as a

form of mere emotional satisfaction that can be constructed in any way or modified at will. (66)

The individualism of our postmodern and globalized era favors a lifestyle which weakens the development and stability of personal relationships and distorts family bonds. (67)

Throughout the document Pope Francis stresses the importance of culture, for believing as individuals is not enough; there must be, for a healthy society, a shared *cultural* dimension of the faith:

The immense importance of a culture marked by faith cannot be overlooked; before the onslaught of contemporary secularism an evangelized culture, for all its limits, has many more resources than the mere sum total of believers. An evangelized popular culture contains values of faith and solidarity capable of encouraging the development of a more just and believing society, and possesses a particular wisdom which ought to be gratefully acknowledged. (68)

I could go on in this vein but I believe this is enough to show that the most crucial elements of the Exhortation have been largely ignored in the public press. But what of the elements that have attracted the attention of the press, namely the attack on economic liberalism and the condemnation of a certain strain of traditionalism? On the first issue, the press, whether of the left or the right, has completely missed the point, while, on the second, it deserves a more sympathetic reading, even from those of us who feel that we are the targets of the attack.

Nearly every news story that has dealt with the economic aspects of the document has used the phrase "unfettered capitalism." But the odd thing is, neither the term "capitalism" nor the word "unfettered" appear anywhere in the document, much less the phrase. This is not a trivial point, because *if* the document had attacked "unfettered capitalism," it would be implicitly an endorsement of some sort of "fettered" capitalism. But it is not that at all; rather, it is an attack on economic liberalism *per se,* fettered or not.

At base, the Pope is attacking the divorce of ethics and economics:

How many words prove irksome to this system! It is irksome when the question of ethics is raised, when global solidarity is invoked, when the distribution of goods is mentioned, when reference is made to protecting labour and defending the dignity of the powerless, when allusion is made to a God who demands a commitment to justice. At other times these issues are exploited by a rhetoric which cheapens them. Casual indifference in the face of such questions empties our lives and our words of all meaning. (203)

This separation of economics and the moral order, this attempt to treat economics as a physical rather than as a humane science, is at the base of the defenses of Capitalism mounted by Thomas Woods and similar writers. But economics is not a physical science; rather, political economy is the science that deals with a certain class of human relationships that are necessary for the material provisioning of society. As with all human relationships, they are governed by the virtue of justice.

Indeed, the very idea of *economic equilibrium*, the balance of supply and demand that allows for markets to be cleared efficiently, is based on the "demanders" getting an equitable portion of what their labor produces, i.e., the just wage. Absent the just wage, markets cannot be cleared economically and equilibrium must rely on government, either as re-distributor of incomes, consumer of last resort, or as both; or on consumer credit (usury) to supplement buying power. The very sign and measure of the deficiency in the just wage is precisely the amount of government spending and consumer lending necessary to clear the markets. Justice, therefore, is not a mere moral platitude but rather a *practical* principle of economic order. Indeed, all morality is practical, since it deals with action in the world.

I am of the opinion that Pope Francis phrased his attack the way he did in order to prevent his works from suffering the fate of those of Pope John Paul II, and especially of *Centesimus Annus*. That encyclical contained a nearly identical attack on economic liberalism, but the most popular interpretation centered on the reading of one sentence within section 42. This section asks whether capitalism is a good thing or not. John Paul answers that with certain restrictions (a "fettered" capitalism, if you will) it could be, but then he concludes by saying, "[but then] it would perhaps be more appropriate to speak of a 'business economy', 'market economy' or simply 'free economy.'" In other words, when capitalism is good, it isn't capitalism and we shouldn't call it that. Based on that rather thin read, a whole interpretation of *Centesimus Annus* as an "endorsement of capitalism" has sprung up. The message of the encyclical was spun out of existence. This, I think, is an example of what Francis means when he says, "At other times these issues are exploited by a rhetoric which cheapens them."

But what then of the attack on traditionalism? Here, I think, another approach is required, given the harsh rhetoric:

> The other [form of worldliness] is the self-absorbed promethean neopelagianism of those who ultimately trust only in their own powers and feel superior to others because they observe certain rules or remain intransigently faithful to a particular Catholic style from the past. A supposed soundness of doctrine or discipline leads instead to a narcissistic and authoritarian elitism, whereby instead of evangelizing, one analyzes and classifies others, and instead of opening the door to grace, one exhausts his or her energies in inspecting and verifying. In neither case is one really concerned about Jesus Christ or others. These are manifestations of an anthropocentric immanentism. It is impossible to think that a genuine evangelizing thrust could emerge from these adulterated forms of Christianity. (94)

As one author points out, there are at least nine insults, or at least rebukes, contained within this brief passage. And if that is not enough, the next paragraph takes a swipe at adherents of the Latin mass ("an ostentatious preoccupation for the liturgy") and accuses them of being

> without any concern that the Gospel have a real impact on God's faithful people and the concrete needs of the present time. In this way, the life of the Church turns into a museum piece or something which is the property of a select few. (95)

This is especially painful because the traditionalists consider them-selves, not without reason, to be among the most loyal and supportive children of Holy Mother Church. As we say in Texas, "Them's fighting words!" Indeed, it is precisely the impact on the "concrete needs of the present time" that motivates most traditionalists.

That being said, we can all think of strains of supposed "traditional-ism" that do indeed fit this description. Certainly, the *sedevacantists* would qualify. Most traditionalists, of course, are not *"sedes."* Neverthe-less, as one becomes a wanderer around the literature of traditionalism, one cannot help but notice a certain tendency in certain quarters for the *"-ism"* to turn into an *ideology,* and one with a particular political agenda. As with all political ideologies, anything that doesn't advance the agenda is truncated or ignored. And for this particular sort of "tradi-tionalist," the content of that ideology is nothing less than *modernism!* Once outside the bounds of liturgy and the issues of marriage, they tend to be Americanists, glorifying the liberalism that is part of our na-tion's founding (as Chris Ferrara has shown) and adopting economic liberalism as their preferred, nay *required,* economic doctrine. This is the "traditionalism" that easily fades into "conservatism" (of a sort) and becomes a servant of the Republican politics. Thus we have a "tradi-tionalism" which exhibits a certain schizophrenia: it demands people believe on Sunday in principles which it demands they abandon on Monday; the workaday world is severed from the world of the Gospel. This is the essence of modernism.

This, I think, is the "traditionalist" who opposes abortion but who does "little to adequately accompany women in very difficult situations, where abortion appears as a quick solution to their profound anguish, especially when the life developing within them is the result of rape or a situation of extreme poverty" (214). Mr. Ferrara has labeled this a "ca-nard," but his critique is both true and false. It is true when speaking of those in the pro-life movement who spend so much time actually work-ing and praying with women in difficult situations and whose concern is for both the child *and* its mother. But it is false for a certain kind of "political" traditionalist, who in fact has little concern for the child or the mother, but rather for the value of the issue to a certain political agenda. What is presented is a truncated form of the tradition which relies on bits from the past to justify bits of the *status quo.*

But tradition is not really about the past at all; it is not, in any sense, antiquarian. Rather, it is about applying the timeless truths learned in the past to the circumstances of the present moment, and of learning how to express that truth in the current culture, or of reforming that culture so that it can absorb the truth. This is a tremendous task, since we live in enemy-occupied territory. The enemy is not just the liberal state, but a corporate culture which, through a vast propaganda apparatus of the 24/7 mass-media, has normalized the attitudes to human relationships which help to create so many mothers in this situation. That is to say, an authentic traditionalism has to address the whole of the cultural problem; it can't be simply the Republican Party with a Latin gloss.

And that brings us back to where we started, to the Pope's aggressive anti-modernism; to his campaign against secularization, rationalism, relativism, individualism, subjectivism, in short against the whole cultural (or anti-cultural) position known as modernism. In this, we have not an opponent but an ally, and an ally willing to fight—and fight aggressively—on pastoral grounds, on grounds which insist on the Church's role in shaping the culture, and shaping it from top to bottom. It must be remembered that the pastoral always has priority within the Church. The Church is not a machine for producing doctrines, but a community for advancing holiness. Indeed, the Church only delves into doctrine to prevent pastoral problems. For example, it took three or four centuries to work out what we now know to be the most central doctrines on the Trinity and the dual nature of Christ. It did not take that long because the Fathers were particularly slow thinkers, but because they only declared doctrines when there was a pastoral need to do so; when not declaring a doctrine would have created confusion among the faithful. St. Nicholas slaps Arius not over an intellectual dispute, but because of the pastoral disaster that Arianism had become.

This is not to suggest that there are not problematic aspects of the document. For example, should the bishops' conferences really have a doctrinal role greater than that which any bishop already has? (33) Surely the bishop has the responsibility of applying doctrinal positions to local situations, and there is a certain advantage to having all the bishops in an area speak with a unified voice. But in a hierarchical

Church, there are limits to collegiality, and I suspect that limit occurs right around doctrinal formulations.

If this Pope is suspicious of traditionalists, he at least shares our concerns. And it is then our task to demonstrate that his concerns with traditionalism *per se* are misplaced, that we are indeed concerned not with old forms for their own sake, but for the sake of the Gospel, and how it impacts "the concrete needs of our time." Given the success of indult masses, traditional parishes, and the growth of traditional orders of priests and nuns, this in itself shouldn't be much of a task; we are, in fact, in the vanguard of the movement the Pope would like to see take place. And as always, we offer ourselves in service to the Church in union with its Pontiff.

John Médaille is a leading voice for distributist economics, an adjunct instructor of Theology at the University of Dallas, and a retired businessman in Irving, Texas. He has authored the books *The Vocation of Business* and *Toward a Truly Free Market.*

CHURCH

# Why I Avoid Both the Catholic Right and the Catholic Left

The other morning I opened my mailbox to find an email from a well-intentioned soul who had clearly misread my own intentions. "Pope Francis is beginning to lose me. Especially his last (Oct. 1) interview," he wrote. "We must pray especially hard for him." Attached was a link to an anti-Pope screed so full of fear, judgment and hate that I wanted to wash my hands after reading it. "The unrepentant sinners who'll be having abortions, fornicating, using pornography, etc. etc.!"

Catholics who are obsessed with other people's sexual behavior, I always feel, are deeply damaged; keeping sexual wounds or secrets they've not yet been able to share; and/or struggling with or indulging in sexual behavior that goes against the teachings of the Church themselves. If you're remotely free in this area, you simply don't pay that much attention. My own reaction to even the slightest degree of such freedom has always been unalloyed amazement, deep gratitude, and an abiding conviction that there *has* to be a God, because no-one with my self-centered fear, narcissistic craving for attention, and disordered nerves could possibly be refraining from acting out sexually, or any other way, except out of love.

The fact is it's hard to be faithful to the teachings of the Church. We all struggle. We've all, at times, failed, sometimes badly. Let's recognize that we all have emotional baggage, generational wounds, and a heart hemorrhaging to feel useful, needed and loved. Let's not impose more heavy burdens and not lift a finger to help. Let's gather round and encourage and share and support each other in our efforts.

Forcing, shaming, and scolding never convert anyone. Does *Let him who is without sin cast the first stone* ring a bell? No-one knew better than Christ our impulse to project our own sins and shadow side upon the other. That's why Pope Francis says, "Convert you? Proselytism is solemn nonsense. You have to meet people and listen to them."

In order to listen you have to have undergone a very long, very excruciating purification process yourself. I don't mean so much as, or only, purification of your sexual capacity and desire, but of your motives. Of your desperate desire, which you keep hidden from yourself, to convert people not to Christ, but to you—*your* rightness, *your* excellence, *your* ability to smartly annihilate your opponent. You have to keep before you at all times that you're a sinner yourself.

People who pay too much attention to the rules always raise a red flag—not because the rules aren't important but because you can only follow them with any kind of sanity and health out of love, not fear. People who are too over-focused on whether everyone else is following the rules worship an empty cross. They've de-incarnated the rules. They've left out actual human beings.

We're not running a country club here; we're running a trauma ward for the sick of soul and spirit. You don't take a 19-year-old who comes from generations of poverty, addiction, mental illness, sexual, physical and emotional abuse—I see such young men and women in jail all the time—and jeer, "Hey perv, put down the porn! I, who come from loving parents, a solid home life, higher education, money, property, prestige and good teeth, am toeing the line—*why can't you?*" You think, with tears in your eyes, *My God, if I'd been born with such staggering odds stacked against me, I'd probably be a pedophile, a rapist, a murderer, a suicide ....*

The rules are not an end in and of themselves. The rules are simply to guide us into some rough kind of shape so that we can be of maximum use and help *to everyone else.* The rules are to prepare us to give an account of ourselves on the day when Christ separates the sheep from the goats. On the day when He asks, *How kind were you? How humble were you? How much did you love the least of these—because the least of these were me?...*

We discover how much we love him when we are willing to sacrifice ourselves, not by judging the sacrifice of others.

People who are following the rules out of freedom, joy and love do so almost unconsciously. People grounded in the love of the Christ of the Gospels almost automatically act in accord with the teachings of the Church. You won't think about it much, but when you do, you'll realize, I'll be darned, my inner compass is in pretty much complete accord with the Catechism, which is to say, with the letter of Christ. And even better and more miraculous, your inner compass will be in accord with the *spirit* of Christ.

You'll follow the rules and then some. You'll offer up not only your sexuality, but your whole self. You'll go to Mass not just once a week, as "required," but several times a week because there is nowhere on EARTH, in spite of rush hour traffic, ringing cell phones and lame music, you'd rather be. You'll know abortion is wrong and the reward is not just that you get to, say, make a living off your political views; the reward is that your heart will open and you'll start being a "mother" to many. You'll be given a whole lot of hidden responsibility and be invited to provide all kinds of hidden service, in anonymity, for no remuneration and at great cost to yourself. You don't need recognition for that; it's a total gift. You want to recognize *Christ* for giving it to you.

There's no blueprint for that. You have to be willing to strike out into unknown territory, to live always in exile, to refrain from identifying yourself with anything or anyone but Christ. This over-focus on the rules purports to be fierce and bold but strikes me instead as fearfully timid. I always want to ask the rule-obsessed: Why attack the weak? Why not attack the biggest idolaters of the age: those who mistake their country for God? Those who persist in the delusion that, oh, say, the United States is a chosen race, a special people, an idea that has been responsible for untold violence, untold suffering, untold derailed lives, and untold millions of senseless, horrific deaths.

I think Pope Francis is saying, "Let's look at *that* sin." I think he's saying that abortion and contraception and sexual behavior that is less than what would bring us and everyone around us fully alive will stop when war stops, when poverty stops, when we open our fearful, hardened hearts and dare to step out of our very carefully-constructed little boxes ...

*The Pope is dissing our contributions,* some of us are raging. But that's not what he's doing at all. He's saying "Yes, we're clear on our teachings, we live and die by our teachings, but the proof that our love for our teachings is legitimate is that we devote our lives to them with *very little fanfare.*"

If we're promoting the sanctity of the human family out of love, what do we care whether we're sufficiently recognized? If we're trying, at great cost to ourselves, to be faithful to the vows of whatever our station in life happens to be, why would we need our efforts to be validated? If we're trying to be Christ in the world, who cares if we're seen? To be upset because we feel our contribution has been minimized is an attitude that goes against the very core of the Gospels, which are entirely based on being willing to take the *last* place, to lose our lives for His sake in order to find it. When we're with Christ, we have the only consolation, warmth, and recognition we'll ever need. We'll no longer look for the approval of the world. Look what the world did to Him! We'll have total faith that our efforts will bear fruit, maybe not in our lifetime, probably not in any way we'll ever begin to see.

Instead, some of us are running around keening, "What's going to happen to our positions as self-proclaimed 'guardians of the faith?' Who's going to be in charge? *Who's going to spy?"*

Here's some super-Good News: We don't need you to spy any more! We get to look for *new* jobs!: as peacemakers, contemplatives, consolers, listeners, healers, gardeners, activists, architects, liturgists, teachers, musicians, artists, writers, artisans, cooks ... because *someone's* gotta prepare that banquet table ...

The Pope is blowing a huge, huge breath of fresh air through the Church. He is putting the lie to the pursed-lipped elder brother in all of us. He is saying—to all of us—*Without love you have nothing.* He is saying—to all of us—*Come to the living water.* He is saying—to all of us—*Come and see ...*

Thus, I replied to my correspondent:

*Oh the Pope isn't losing me at all! On the contrary, with great courage and to my intense joy, he's corroborating the idea of what it is to be a follower of Christ that I've had all along.*

*I'm going to pray especially hard that he continues in this vein, and I think we should all pray especially hard for our own continuing conversion to the scandalous Christ of the Gospels!*

*I don't bother myself with the kind of voices in the links you sent—I so appreciate your goodwill but please don't pass on such material again.*

And now—let's eat!

Heather King is a writer and speaker with several memoirs, among them *Parched; Redeemed; Shirt of Flame;* and *Poor Baby.* Her writing appears monthly in *Magnificat* and weekly in *Aleteia* and *The Tidings,* and she blogs at heather-king.com. She lives in Los Angeles.

# Taking Augustine as Guide

When I met Augustine it disrupted everything. I was assigned the *Confessions* in an English class at Brandeis University entitled *Literature and Heresy*. Before then I had skimmed it in high school, but the translation had been so idiosyncratic and archaic all the poetry had been obscured. In the squeaking linoleum halls of my suburban Texan public school Augustine read like an imperious preacher, scolding and scorning.

By the time I read him again as a sophomore, his voice was *sonorous*. With a foreword by the venerable Peter Brown and translation by F. J. Sheed, the lyricism of the *Confessions* stunned me, changed everything. I put aside the rest of my reading for that course and wrote only on him for our assignments. In discussion I listened intently, and with every comment my peers made my mind reeled: there was just so *much* to him, such intricacy in every argument, I could barely think of anything to say. My professor noticed the fixation but didn't probe too much; I got the impression she was glad someone was doing the assigned reading in at least one of the texts.

I was doing more than reading him; I just wasn't sure what.

✳ ✳ ✳

In retrospect I had a hard time identifying the development taking place within me for precisely the same reason Augustine had during his conversion, though my context prevented me from seeing it then. Among my friends and family and the things they all knew me to be—a lifelong protestant, for one—it was difficult for me to make sense of what use I could have for a saint. What more could Augustine ever be to me, and the unified Catholic church he advocated, besides quaint historical artifacts or, more tantalizingly, a glimpse of a life over a fence I knew with full confidence I could never surmount?

Of course, this is precisely the sort of thing Augustine himself went through in the process of his own conversion. Manichaeanism admittedly provided quite a stark contrast with his burgeoning Catholicism compared to my southern Protestantism, but the effect was essentially the same: prior to conversion, Augustine was radically alone.

This is part of what makes the pre-conversion narrative of his *Confessions* so compelling; his thoughts read like a modern novel, overwhelming in intimacy and insight. Charles Taylor is right to note that "Augustine makes the step toward inwardness ... because it is a step toward God," and in no place is his command of inward thought so intensely evident as in the almost claustrophobically revealed first half of his *Confessions*.

But there is a distinction to be drawn between inwardness in pursuit of truth and therefore God, and inwardness that seeks itself alone. The latter is the sort that produced in the young Augustine a tumultuous solitude, a bondage forged from "the iron of [his] own will." The degree to which Augustine was at that time ensnared with his own desires is one of the most striking features of *Confessions*, building into the climax of his conversion:

> ... It was I. I did not wholly will, I was not wholly unwilling. Therefore I strove with myself and was distracted by myself.

Christ occasions the turn from an inwardness marked by self-seeking to an inwardness paradoxically open to communion with others. While Augustine's conversion frees him from his lust, it does not leave him solitary and self-reliant, but rather enmeshed in community:

> ... I could see the austere beauty of Continence, serene and indeed joyous but not evilly, honorably soliciting me to come

to her and not linger, stretching forth loving hands to receive and embrace me, hands full of multitudes of good examples. With her I saw such hosts of young men and maidens, a multitude of youth of every age, gray widows and women grown old in virginity, and in them all Continence herself, not barren but the fruitful mother of children.

The self turned inward without the light of God finds a mire, becomes its own enslavement. But the self turned inward in search of God is joined by others on that same journey: this is the revelation Augustine comes to in conversion. And through it the oppressive storm of his self-battling breaks; he breathes the good air, joins his friend in a garden, and the rest, as they say, is history.

What occurred to me again and again as I read and re-read the *Confessions* was this sense of a thoroughgoing community: I could see that I wanted it, I knew that I needed it to continue on, but I couldn't logically work out how I might be united with Christians globally, or those who had died before my birth.

What bound us together, really? In the multitudes of exemplary Christians who had come before him, Augustine glimpsed a source of shared strength available thanks to a shared love, and in him I began to see the same. It just took some time for me to figure out how to affirm and draw upon it, because the radical is often simple: like Augustine, I needed to dispense with the interior conflicts, look upward before inward, and come to the Catholic Church.

And, like Augustine, it took a good while and much encouragement for me to make my move.

* * *

Eventually I began to suspect my interest in Augustine bordered on the pathological. Having the language of devotion unavailable to me (indeed, it would've veered toward the idolatrous to suggest such a thing in my hard-nosed Methodist family) I decided to translate my passion into the language my upbringing provided: that of vocation. I would make a profession of theology, which would provide a comfortable academic backdrop to sterilize what was for me swiftly developing into full-blown love.

173

It turns out becoming a theologian isn't what it once was; I get the sense a point in time existed where one could do a suitable amount of reading and hang out a *theologian* shingle. Not so anymore. I needed, I realized, to go to graduate school, and my search for the elusive duo of admittance and funding brought me eventually to the University of Cambridge in the United Kingdom, far from my home in Texas.

At no point did it occur to me that estrangement would change my spirituality. This is in part because I wasn't out to get away, exactly; it was also because I was and remain very close to my family and home, and don't hold either of them accountable for keeping me from anything. But nonetheless it was at Cambridge that, after a long day of slogging through texts for our dissertations, a friend of mine closed her book and in the fading light of the Divinity library sighed: "I love Augustine."

And this love *wasn't* the love of cheesecake or Rihanna or *True Detective* or any of the other hundreds of things we say we love when we mean enjoy. Not that there isn't a little love in enjoyment; but the point stands: when my friend said she loved Augustine, she meant it. And I knew that I did, too.

Which doesn't seem like the sort of revelation that should be shattering, but it was. For a little while I thought I was just silly; plenty of girls love characters in books in some sense—I shudder to invoke *Twilight's* Edward Cullen, but the thought did occur to me—but Augustine is never merely a character in his writing; he's always over and above it. He is a *guide*. As Peter Candler writes in *Theology, Rhetoric, and Manuduction: or Reading Scripture Together on the Path to God:*

> For here theology is not understood as the probative demonstration of the truth of the Christian faith, of God's existence, or of the resurrection of the body, but primarily as the practice of the proper ordering of one's will … toward its object. The practice of reading, therefore, is the "art" of conforming one's will to the likeness of Christ, by virtue of the "baptism" of understanding, which is transformed into wisdom, indeed, the very wisdom of God himself, the Son of God.

Augustine's theology had changed me, but the change was bound up with him, with his guidance, with his life. And at the time I wasn't sure how to cope with it, how to answer the call of a church so full of voices their clarity proposed to me above the din of what I was so *sure* of previously: that there was no such thing as intercession, that the dead are wholly beyond us, that our final relationship with God is marked by solitude.

But the voices of the many finally soothed the voice of this one.

\* \* \*

Augustine's "law of love" is the law of Christ, a foundational principle that precedes and founds all other ethics. This is not to say that love is a kind of litmus test for ethical prescription in the way that contemporary Christians will often in a slippery sense promote it; but rather to say that the love of Christ poses the question that necessitates all ethics. What is it that you love? Augustine supposes there are really only two answers: the self or God.

But with the love of God comes so much, in part because that love is finally, gloriously requited. When one loves God, one is entitled to love all that which God has given, and to love it truly, foundationally, purely. This is what Augustine calls "rightly ordered love," and it's that love the Church is here to facilitate and serve.

The reason Augustine calls the Catholic Church "the unity" is precisely because all who love God are in communion together; their right love enables them to love another wholly, and in their love they work together to come closer to Christ, to know Him better, love him all the more. Because rightly ordered love requires the education of the moral conscience and the support of others to continue growing, the Catholic Church becomes a vast extended family, all of us offering up helping hands on our shared journey. Even those who have passed on and now reside eternally can help us, provided we pray: "for the souls of the pious dead are not separated from the Church, which even now is in the kingdom of Christ."

Augustine is often cast as having a sort of fanatical devotion to Catholic unity, to the point of advocating the state persecution of heretics, most notably the Donatists. It's easy to read him with a cynical eye for his project of unification, but as I read him as a graduate student I began to see the grandeur of it: through the same law of love, Augustine argued for continuity between the living church and those who have gone on before, and also for equality between those who viewed themselves as church elite and those who thought they could never aspire to such a station. We're united, Augustine says, by our love: "we have learned that there is a City of God, and its Founder has inspired us with a love which makes us covet its citizenship."

Love for Augustine was, therefore, an invitation. In my estrangement from the things that had over time deafened my heart to the echoes of love all around me—in those I saw, the things I read, the images and icons I study—I found the quietude to accept.

On Easter of 2014, I was received into the Catholic Church. Even now the story of *why*—which I know is of curious interest to family and friends—has a mystical bent to it, and reads as a little eccentric. *You became Catholic because you loved Augustine?* Not precisely: I became Catholic because I love God, and only in the Catholic imagination could my love of Augustine grow into an encounter that lights the way to better love of God. This is the very stuff, I think, of the *culture of authentic encounter* Pope Francis is now doing the work of developing to its fullness, and if his aim is a new evangelism then in this case he's succeeded. As Augustine initially saw, love founds community: to reach out in love is to encounter authentically, and to extend the greatest of invitations. This ethic is the law of love, and "love is the fulfillment of the law."

Elizabeth Stoker Bruenig is working toward her Ph.D. in religion and politics at Brown University. She has an M.Phil. in Christian Theology from the University of Cambridge. When she isn't reading Augustine, she is working in her garden.

# The Migrant and the Latin Church

The election of Pope Francis was a first for many things. It was a first for nomenclature, marking the first papal use of the name "Francis," leading to a brief debate on whether Francis I was the proper title to grant the new Pontiff. It was a first for religious life, with a Jesuit wearing the Fisherman's ring, leading to the tongue in cheek remarks on whether this Jesuit pope had to swear obedience to himself. What caught the media's attention—and by extension ours—however, at the time of his election was the fact that this was a first for geographic shifts. Not only was the Pope non-Italian (though of Italian descent), but he was a Pope from the Global South, more specifically, the Archbishop of Buenos Aires in Argentina.

Though there have been a significant list of Pope's coming from countries other than Italy—the Polish John Paul II and the German Benedict XVI being the latest additions to this list—an inclusion from outside the familiar boundaries of Europe brings into sharper relief a growing trend hinted at in Philips Jenkins' books *The Next Christendom*. This trend is the emergence of the Catholic Church as the Church of migrants. A visit by Pope Francis early in his papacy to the Italian island of Lampedusa, an infamous point of entry for irregular migrant entry from North Africa into Europe, makes it clear that migrants are, if not the central issue, certainly is not a tangential concern for the Church.

Also Indicative of this growing attention to migrants is the experience of the Church within the United States. A 2008 Pew Forum on Religion and Public Life indicated that whilst one in four American adults leave the faith of their childhood, Catholicism's numbers within the United States have been kept stable by an influx of migrants into the parishes, with some states experiencing growth in adherents as high as 50% percent between 1990 and 2000. While these changes within the United States will no doubt change the face of American Catholicism, it is also important to note how this fits into a much larger pattern of change within Roman Catholicism globally. There is also the question of what role that the migrant would play in this transition.

Below are two broad areas of consideration, which then branch out into a number of more specific points. It should be noted from the outset that reflections on these implications are spoken from the particularly of a denizen of the Latin Church from Australia (a migrant to that land, and living in the United States at the time of writing). Though the most numerous and visible portion of the Church, the Latin Church should be considered as only one aspect of the much larger discussion of the other rites which together make up the Catholic Church.

## Global Topoi in Roman Catholicism

One of the most apparent changes to consider is the shifts in Roman Catholicism's demographic centre of gravity, a shift that would dilute the association of Christianity generally—Roman Catholicism in particular—with the West. The Pew Forum mentioned above, the sociologist Philip Jenkins[1] and the historian Lamin Sanneh[2] provide strong evidence that over the past century, Christianity's Euro-American privilege has very decisively declined. In France and Germany, Cathedrals are emptying out and becoming increasingly used for con-

---

[1] Philip Jenkins, *The Next Christendom: The Coming of Global Christianity*, 3rd edition (Oxford ; New York: Oxford University Press, 2011).

[2] Lamin Sanneh, *Whose Religion Is Christianity?: The Gospel beyond the West* (Grand Rapids, Mich: Wm. B. Eerdmans Publishing Co., 2003).

certs or museum exhibits rather than places of worship. Meanwhile, new vital centres of Christianity are emerging in Asia, Latin America and Africa. Jenkens estimates that by 2030, there will be more Catholics in Africa than Europe. Another indicator is the Philippines, which with its over 72 million adherents, already has more Roman Catholics than some European nations have citizens. The overall pattern seems to indicate that the Spirit is moving the Church's centre of gravity away from the more affluent West to the relatively more populous and economically disadvantaged nations in what is broadly called "the Global South."

The implications of this shift are much more subtle than just the simplistic claim that the Church as an institution of the West is finished. The considerable incubation period within this milieu means that its monastic and intellectual heritage (the great doctors of the Church like Aquinas and Bonaventure), as well as liturgical traditions (the Latin Rites such as the Roman) will continue to endure in these new centers of an increasingly global Roman Catholicism. They might develop and adjust, but the strong family resemblance will surely remain. What will change considerably is the way in which this heritage is made, and will be made, to speak to the joys, hopes and anxieties that are unique to the peoples within these centres. From a seemingly unified voice emanating from the West, what may appear would be an array of geographically, culturally and socially conditioned voices speaking from within the same Church, a vivid reminder of the many parts that make up the Body of Christ (Rom 12:5).

There will be a challenge concerning how to render a potential cacophony into a harmonics with this multiplication of voices within the particularity of the Latin Church. With this broadening of voices would surely come a broadening of the concerns of the Church qua Church. Whether one likes it or not, the papacy of Francis will be one where the culture wars will not be confined to the programs set by media and political elites, one speaks here of sexual mores within the Church. The contours of the culture war might expand to bring other questions closer to the center of the Church's pastoral agenda. It will also be about whether the Church can countenance socioeconomic processes that are currently in place in a global economy, that have in the main resulted in growing economic inequality, untold poverty-induced suffering, and environmental catastrophe. *Evangelii Gaudium,* which has attracted "Holy Father, you are wrong's" from many within Catholicism, already bears out the discomfort that this broadened range of concerns will generate. This challenge is upon us already, but pretending that such an array of voices is not there is foolish.

## Migrant Church

Another cliché that is often touted is how the migrant will emphasise the migrant status of the Church. Usually, popular take ups of this theme would go something like "the migrant moves around, so the church will move around too," or that "Jesus was a migrant, so migrants are important for the Church," or more substantially, that "the migrant reminds us that the Church is on pilgrimage to heaven." All these may be true in at one level, but a more interesting question would be the implications of affirming this pilgrim status on the everyday life of the Roman Catholic.

One effect that the migrant brings that one might not consider is the centrality of the transformative personal encounter as the locus of redemption (something long advocated by the late founder of the ecclesial movement called Communion and Liberation, Luigi Giussani) rather than the collapse of redemption with an adherence to a code of law or a schema of position statements. This is important because the migrant is someone of whom understanding is borne out by a personal encounter with a stranger, rather than a depersonalised statistic or a demographic. Yet, for too long the only understanding of the migrant has been filtered through the language of gauging by their ability to become "law-abiding citizens," which has more often than not become code for an ability to dovetail with set policy agendas. Or to put it more bluntly, we acknowledge the migrant to the extent that "they" become like "us." This trend has often been met by the counter-demand from migrants for recognition of their unique status as persons, even in ways that would not compute with the law at a given time. In a similar fashion, the Catholic migrant should draw to our attention that salvation is more like the story of the Samaritan woman at the well in the Gospel of John (4:1–26), where redemption means a revelatory encounter with Jesus which is passed on to others, rather than the parabolic Pharisee who equates his redeemed status with his observance of the law. In other words, redemption is less about counting the number of strikes, than it is about, as Pope Francis once said in his interview with Antonio Spadaro, being transformed by a face to face encounter between God and a sinner.

Reconsidering the primacy of the encounter between sinner and God, instantiated in our day in the encounter with the migrant should cause us to reconsider—or rather retrieve—the role of the Church as a textured Body of Christ. In an essay presented in Washington, Luigi Giussani likened the Church to the garments of Jesus that children who encountered him clung to. In the same way that tiny children encountered Jesus via his Body (rather than the sight of His face), the Church is not a stale institution, but the living means by which that same Body comes to be made present for us to cling to.3 With this turn to the Church as the site of encountering, and being converted by, the living God comes also a turn away from the notion of Christianity as a series of positions statements. This turn towards the encounter with the living God is at once something that simplifies (because the primary concern for the Christian shifts to one of being converted by the gaze of a loving God) and complexifies (because the implications of that conversion force us to cut across and go beyond any one set of policies, positions and parties).

The primacy of a *transformative* encounter between the sinner and God should also cause us to consider how our pilgrimage on earth would be a series of transformations that come every time with every renewed encounter in every stage in history. This should knock us out of our complacent association of Christianity with presumptions that we see as natural givens for the Christian life, whether those givens be the monarchy, the free market, baroque architecture, empire, conservatism and the like. At the heart of this presumption of what is a proper Christian life is the presumption that one knows the Christian life in its totality. You can count on a migrant to challenge the degree to which one knows everything as a Catholic, or remind us the degree to which

---

3  Giussani, "Tu" (o dell'amicizia). *The Religious Sense Symposium: Person, Meaning and Culture in America.* September 1998, Georgetown University Conference Center, Washington DC.

we "know in part" (1 Cor 13:9). Indeed, Augustine cautions us about our pretensions concerning complete knowledge of anything in Book IV of his *Confessions*. Think you know the whole, Augustine writes, and you only betray the partial nature of your knowledge.4

For the Catholic migrant, his or her Catholicism cannot help but be intertwined with his or her nomadic experience and multiple belonging. What this testifies to is not a "foreign" incursion on the older, more natural, Western Catholicism. Rather, what this testifies to are the implications of Christ's mandate to disciple all the nations. The Great Commission will mean that as the Gospel (and by extension, Catholicism) belongs in all places, Catholicism's testament to the encounter with Christ will necessarily sound out *from* all places. As it does so, our attention will be drawn to two things.

First, the migrant embodies this belonging to all places primarily in his or her multiple belonging, professing an affiliation with one's place of birth as well as domicile, and often struggle to reconcile these affiliations. This multiple belonging is not a fault that only migrants have, as if the native-born Catholic need only worry of his singular affiliation to Catholicism. The seeming multiplicity of the migrant in a way mirrors the multiplicity that is in each and every one of us. They remind all of us, once again, of what Augustine counseled the early Church. In the same way that Augustine warns that our protestations of knowledge betray our partial knowledge, so does he warn that our protestations of having a unity of desire and heart betray our multiplicity in reality, as we often profess our united love for God whilst directing our desires towards causes other than God, substituting our friendship with God with a chauvinistic enthusiasm for causes, campaigns or country, even when done in God's name.

The second thing that a migrant's multiple belonging testifies to is the way that each member of this array of voices that would sound out the Testament of Jesus will have unique accents. Each new inflection that these accents bring will inevitably challenge any privileged, Euro-American, version of Catholicism. They may be important and formative adaptations whose influence will (and sometimes should) be long

---

4 Augustine, *The Confessions*, Book IV, Chapter 11

felt, but one can too easily romanticise and fetishize them to the status of Divine Revelation, which justifies an ossifying of these adaptations that will render Divine Revelation inaccessible to those outside a self-appointed cultural elite. Another aspect of the challenge that the Church of the migrant unearths, however, is the degree to which it is easy also to fetishize the contingent accent of the Gospel and make that trump the universality of the Gospel itself, thereby making identity, rather than the Gospel, the paramount concern.

## Conclusion

If there is one question that sums up the issues outlined above, it would be: "How does one be simultaneously a Global Catholic in the Latin Church?" This single question, though abstract, then branches out to an array of more practical concerns both for the Catholic migrant, and the Church as a whole. For the migrant, the question would concern how it would be possible to refract the Roman-ness of one's Catholicism through one's own, quintessentially non-Roman, migrant experiences. For the Church, the question would relate to the identity of things that were once considered indispensable to Catholicism but were merely historically contingent accretions, and what to do with these accretions in the face of others coming from elsewhere.

Both questions are not easy to answer, and together these challenges will persist so long as the Church reflects the journey of the Son of Man, who had no place to rest his head (Lk 9:58), yet stands at each door and knocks so that He may commune with us (Rev 3:20). As the migrant lives in a land that is not his or hers, the Church on this side of the *eschaton* moves within a space that is not hers. Rather than a source of anxiety, the lack of triumphalistic control that comes with recognising the migrant status of the Church ought to be an occasion of light-heartedness. Or to borrow from Michel de Certeau's *Practice of Everyday Life*, the Church's migrant status ought to introduce the notion of a lighthearted dance through these spaces controlled by the "powers and principalities of this world," just as we see the lighthearted displays of dance and song in a migrant's life in a new country, bringing life to both migrant and country.

Matthew Tan is the Felice and Mar-
gredel Zaccari Lecturer in Theology
and Philosophy at Campion College
in Sydney, Australia. He has also
been Visiting Assistant Professor in
Catholic Studies and a Research Fellow in the Center for World Catholicism and Intercultural Theology in
DePaul University in Chicago. His
recent book is *Justice, Unity and the
Hidden Christ: The Theopolitical Complex of the Social Justice Approach to
Ecumenism* (Pickwick, 2014). He is
the editor of the theological blog *The
Divine Wedgie*—divinewedgie.blog-
spot.com.

# Priests and Prophets, Centers and Peripheries

*Do you know the story of the drunken man who crossed the Place de la Concorde at night? He knocked against the railing that surrounds the obelisk and went round and round until morning; he thought he was locked in.* [1]

Take this story, get the image in your head, and then replace the "railing that surrounds the obelisk" and imagine the outer walls of a church. Think, too, a bit about parish boundaries, as that will be helpful. And now take the *spatial* idea of a circle that surrounds an obelisk and convert it to a *temporal* metaphor and think of the railing as surrounding that hour or hour-and-a-half that constitutes the normal, Catholic, Sunday mass and I think we can go a long way toward an understanding of Pope Francis on the frequently misunderstood "sin" of clericalism, one of the major themes of his pontificate. This sin is really a about a polar relationship between centers and peripheries that, according to the Pope, often fall

---

[1] Sulivan, Jean. *Morning Light.* Paulist Press, 1988.

out of balance. Being out of balance is another form of "missing the mark," which is a common definition of sin.

In contrast with the emphases of many Popes, and instead of always pointing the finger of blame at the outside culture for the current woes of the Church—the regular complaints about relativism, secularism, and lethargy—Francis has espoused an inward, non-codependent focus on trouble, often dressing down church leadership (with himself included), while simultaneously asking for a mission-centered church. It's a dynamic and mature worldview that is misunderstood by those who think statically and who often work, unawares, at purposes directly counter to this double movement. Clericalism, according to his diagnosis, is one of the problems working against this vision and it is actually, he says, a "double-sin" in that "priests take pleasure in the temptation to clericalize the laity, but many of the laity are on their knees asking to be clericalized, because it is more comfortable, it is more comfortable!"[2]

The laity are on their knees asking to be clericalized; the drunk man thinks he's locked in when he's actually free. What the drunk man and many lay people in the Church have in common are stupors of one kind or another, misunderstanding, self-imposed lack of mobility, and a form of immaturity. The upshot is that, shorn of any balancing factor, the Church laity often tends to exist in a sort of "disabled" condition that Ivan Illich (a man who understood centers and peripheries) saw in the community-destroying, passive, consumer mentality cultivated by most "professions." In fact, according to Illich's analysis, a certain form the Catholic priesthood adopted in the age of Charlemagne was the prototypical "disabling profession." This was when the role of the priest got merged with the role of the pastor.

Professions become disabling when they take on the executive, legislative and judicial functions, all in one, and begin to impute needs to their clients that create dependencies for their services which, in many cases, can be done quite well by the clients themselves. In an analogy of this, the man in the story was magnetized by what was on the inside

---

[2] "Address to Members of the 'Corallo' Association," March 22, 2014.

with the obelisk and, in his stupor, he failed to recognize the all the freedom he actually did have and was acting in a disabled condition.

Pope Francis elaborates on this theme, the confusion of the correct relationship between centers and peripheries which exists in the Church:

> When there is a lay person who does a good job and is committed, their parish priest goes to the local bishop—and this happened to me in Buenos Aires—and says: "Why don't we make him a deacon?" This is a mistake: if we have a good lay person, let him carry on being just that." ("Corallo" Address)

And, in *Evangelii Gaudium,* he writes

> Even if many are now involved in the lay ministries, this involvement is not reflected in a greater penetration of Christian values in the social, political and economic sectors. It often remains tied to tasks within the Church, without a real commitment to applying the Gospel to the transformation of society. (102)

This makes me think of the disservice I've always felt going on around me when, instructing youth for Confirmation, we let them know that, with this Sacrament, they are now adults in the Church and can serve as a "Greeter," or a "Lector," when really, according to Francis, the emphasis on mature Catholic adulthood is about going outside the walls/the parish/the "railings" and being leaven in a world desperately in need of the Gospel.

Now this story of the obelisk is not obtained from just anywhere. It's an anecdote found in the writings of Jean Sulivan, (1913–1980), a French Catholic writer (with, sadly, too few of his books translated into English), whom Joseph Cunneen called "The most significant writer of Christian inspiration in France since George Bernanos." Sulivan was a priest released from his duties by the Cardinal of Paris in order to focus full-time on writing. He had a foot in two worlds and he, too, understood centers and peripheries. In my reading, Sulivan is the Catholic thinker that Pope Francis most resembles—a true kindred spirit—and this story of the obelisk is set in the context of a discussion on the need for a free imagination in thinking about the future of the Church, which is stifled when there is a veritable obsession with the issues pertaining to the Sanctuary (read: obelisk). In fact, the coda which follows this story says: "Except in a scientific or technical field, *any constraint on thinking is already a deception.* This is all the more true when it pretends to present *God's message.*" (Emphasis mine.)

Here, then, in this addendum, we have an oblique reference to prophets, "God's messengers," whom Pope Francis claims can balance out the clericalism in the Church:

A church without prophets falls into the trap of clericalism. ... True prophets hold within themselves three different moments: past, present, and future. They keep the promise of God alive, they see the suffering of their people, and they bring us the strength to look ahead. When there is no prophecy amongst the people of God, the emptiness that is created gets filled by clericalism. All memory of the past and hope for the future are reduced only to the present: no past promise, no future hope. But when clericalism reigns supreme the words of God are sorely missed, and true believers weep because they cannot find the Lord. (Homily, December 12, 2013)

I am not a prophet, more of a dullard, but I think a lot about centers and peripheries as I am a layman who is appointed as leader of my local Catholic parish due to a shortage of priests, according to Canon 517.2. It's a strange role in that I often feel that 50% of my peers see my role primarily as a layman who's somehow gotten himself over the "railings that surround the obelisk" and should be vying for more visibility in the liturgy as part of the cause of an abstract justice. The other 50% are dumbfounded that, being a male, I refused to just pick up an ordination to the diaconate on the quick so as to preach and to touch the holy vessels. In response, I often hear myself saying that I prefer to put my focus on, and represent, the hundreds of square miles in our parish that are *not* the Church building and those other 167 hours in the week that are *not* the Sunday liturgy, all the while knowing that I probably won't be understood.

My goal and my prayer, however, is to use my somewhat liminal role to create a space for prophets and saints to arise and be noticed in our rural parish. They, after all, as anyone who studies Church history knows, will constitute the real renewal of the Church, and one must presume that Pope Francis knows that too. As I see it, it's our job to hear his proclamation and put it into practice, else the message can turn against itself and lead to other, more insidious, forms of apathy.

In one of the paradoxes of Pope Francis' pontificate, and contrary to his very real attempt to symbolize and say, "It's not about me," there's a strand of the Pope's popularity (think of the term "Poparazzi") that encourages a mirror-image of the clericalism he's trying so hard to fight. He's a rock star of sorts, and so quotable, and so there's a temptation to let him make all the changes, while we pray for him, sit back, and watch. I can hear the Poparazzi saying, regarding this spectatorial stance, as if they were in a movie theater: "It's more comfortable. It's more comfortable." And yet this stance is but another, more subtle, version of the same disease.

Like the therapist tying to enable and set free her client who has become dependent on her ministrations, the way toward freedom always has a gravitational pull working against it. In other words, this clericalism thing is a slippery fish, and without vigilance it's easy to fall into the pattern where one casts out one demon only to find that seven others have come to take its place, "and the last state of that man is worse than the first" (Matt. 12:45).

I do not intend to suggest that the way towards freedom is solely in a correct understanding of priests and prophets, centers and peripheries (as, in my analysis, I've studiously avoided even mentioning the role of "kings"). But our culture is so utterly dominated by behavior learned in theaters, stadiums and screens, which have their own passive, "spectatorial" dynamic between centers and peripheries quite opposed to the one I'm trying to elucidate here, that I think highlighting this theme is useful. By its nature, it can't be fully accomplished from the top down, and to that end I'll complete these reflections with a few references to a few prophets and prophetic *logoi spermatikoi* that I believe can help complement the words and directives coming from Pope Francis. I honestly believe that, without getting this renewed vision of Vatican II that Francis is offering, the whole thing could come to naught.

1. Ivan Illich's *Disabling Professions* (2000) is an acute analysis of this theme. He is developing insights in this book that were first put forth in an essay called "The Vanishing Clergyman" (1967), where he warned that too narrow a focus on women's ordination and married clergy might work to further entrench this spectatorial mode of doing Church. Instead, though never seeing the disappearance of the priesthood, he envisioned a future church that might have more the characteristic of, "the face-to-face meeting of families around a table, rather than the impersonal attendance of a crowd around an altar."3

2. Charles Williams, one of the famed "Inkings" and a prophetic character himself, frequently made reference to a maxim of great significance that he attributed to the poet Coventry Patmore: "The distance between an ordinary meal and that nourishment that is communicated in the Eucharist should lessen, as it were, until perhaps to the devout soul every meal is an actual Eucharist."4

3. On the role of the prophet, I've read nothing better than Martin Buber's *The Prophetic Faith*. Buber focuses his penetrating insight into the relationships of prophets and priests: "Centralization and codification, undertaken in the interests of religion, are a danger to the core of religion, unless there is the strongest life of faith, embodied in the whole existence of the community, and not relaxing in its renewing activity." And, maybe hearkening to our Church in the future, when the poles of the relationship meet in the middle, he says, "The true *nabi* (prophet) ... is the true priest."5

4. And, in terms of piety, I think there's nothing more symbolic and prophetic than the message of Fatima regarding prayer to the Immaculate Heart of Mary. It seems to echo the principle, in physics, of harmonic resonance, whereby an infinitesimal force applied at

---

3 *Celebration of Awareness: A Call for Institutional Revolution.* Garden City, NY: Doubleday & Company, Inc., 1970. p. 69.

4 *Outlines of Romantic Theology,* Erdmans, 1990, pg. 9.

5 Buber, Harper Torchbooks, 1949. pg. 170 & 62.

the center can shape huge forces at the periphery. Everybody, whether inside the railings or not, can practice this prayer for the world as a discipline of the universal priesthood. The most remarkable modern example of this force is the nearly unbelievable survival of eight Jesuits whose home was only eight blocks from "ground zero" of the atomic bomb dropped on Hiroshima in 1945. When interviewed on American television and asked to account for this apparent miracle, one of the survivors responded: "In that house, we were living the message of Fatima."[6]

To echo Jean Sulivan once again: *"Any constraint on thinking is already a deception."* Pope Francis is doing his part. Now we must do ours.

Michael J. Sauter is a married father of four living in up-state New York. He serves as Pastoral Administrator of St. Luke the Evangelist Parish and as Director of Catholic Campus Ministry at SUNY Geneseo, where he also adjuncts in Humanities.

---

[6] Johnston, Francis, *Fatima: The Great Sign*, TAN Publishers, 1980, p. 139

# Freedom to Take the Form of a Slave: Toward a Kenotic Ecclesiology

## The False Doctrine of Power

In the final chapter of J. R. R. Tolkien's *The Fellowship of the Ring*, Boromir, one of those accompanying the quest to destroy the corrupting One Ring, finally succumbs to the lust for its power. He reasons under its influence to the appointed ring-bearer Frodo:

> "Yet may I not even speak of it? For you seem ever to think only of its power in the hands of the Enemy: of its evil uses not of its good. The world is changing, you say, Minas Tirith will fall, if the Ring lasts. But why? Certainly, if the Ring were with the Enemy. But why, if it were with us?"
>
> "Were you not at the Council?" answered Frodo. "Because we cannot use it, and what is done with it turns to evil."
>
> Boromir got up and walked about impatiently. "So you go on," he cried. "Gandalf, Elrond—all these folk have taught you to say so. For themselves they may be right. These elves and half-elves and wizards, they would come to grief perhaps. Yet often I doubt if they are wise and not merely timid.

But each to his own kind. True-hearted Men, they will not be corrupted. We of Minas Tirith have been staunch through long years of trial. We do not desire the power of wizard-lords, only strength to defend ourselves, strength in a just cause. And behold! in our need chance brings to light the Ring of Power. It is a gift, I say; a gift to the foes of Mordor. It is mad not to use it, to use the power of the Enemy against him. The fearless, the ruthless, these alone will achieve victory. What could not a warrior do in this hour, a great leader? What could not Aragorn do? Or if he refuses, why not Boromir? The Ring would give me power of Command. How I would drive the hosts of Mordor, and all men would flock to my banner!"

Boromir strode up and down, speaking ever more loudly. Almost he seemed to have forgotten Frodo, while his talk dwelt on walls and weapons, and the mustering of men; and he drew plans for great alliances and glorious victories to be; and he cast down Mordor, and became himself a mighty king, benevolent and wise. Suddenly he stopped and waved his arms.

"And they tell us to throw it away!" he cried. "I do not say destroy it. That might be well, if reason could show any hope of doing so. It does not. The only plan that is proposed to us is that a halfling should walk blindly into Mordor and offer the Enemy every chance of recapturing it for himself. Folly!"

Woven throughout Tolkien's heroic tale is the thread of strength made perfect in weakness, to borrow St. Paul's phrasing. And indeed such a counter-intuitive strength has often appeared as folly, even among those who would seek to further its mission. What could be more foolish, we are tempted to think, than refusing to wield any available means of "strength in a just cause"—and what cause could be more just than the mission of the Church? And yet if we are to take any lesson from Boromir's fall, it is that the true folly is in thinking ourselves incorruptible by power in its more obvious—and impatient—forms. This is why the erstwhile marginalization that Catholics have sometimes faced (I am thinking particularly of the Catholic experience in 19th-century America), despite a long-standing impulse to strain against it, is a great blessing in disguise for the Catholic Church. It is also why we need an ecclesiology (specifically in the *ad extra* sense) built on the Church's founding event: the passion, death, and resurrection of our Lord Jesus Christ.

Karl Rahner once wrote of the Church as the "Real Symbol" of the presence of Christ on earth, just as Christ was of the Father,[1] and the lectionary readings we hear in the liturgy of Palm Sunday and the Paschal Triduum provide a Christological foundation for thinking about how we collectively—that is, as Church—can live up to that distinction. As we begin Holy Week we hear a model of Christ's *kenosis,* or self-emptying, in the ancient hymn preserved by St. Paul in his letter to the Philippians:

> Christ Jesus, though he was in the form of God,
> did not regard equality with God
> something to be grasped.
> Rather, he emptied himself,
> taking the form of a slave,
> coming in human likeness;
> and found human in appearance,
> he humbled himself,
> becoming obedient to the point of death,
> even death on a cross.
> Because of this, God greatly exalted him
> and bestowed on him the name
> which is above every name,
> that at the name of Jesus
> every knee should bend,
> of those in heaven and on earth and under the earth,
> and every tongue confess that

---

[1] "Theology of the Symbol," *Theological Investigations IV.* It must be noted that a Rahnerian understanding of "symbol" is completely contrary to a weaker connotation of the word as suggesting *mere* representation: a "Real Symbol," rather, makes actually present what it signifies.

Jesus Christ is Lord,
to the glory of God the Father.

## The Church as Public Power, or Public Witness?

The idea that Christ's glory-in-humility is to be imitated by his fol-
lowers is present even in the immediate context of Paul's letter, in
which he introduces this hymn of praise by exhorting the Philippian
Christians, "Let the same mind be in you ...." A kenotic ecclesiology,
then, should follow naturally from this kenotic Christology. What does
it mean for the Church to take "the form of a slave" to the world, refusing to grasp at power, as her very Lord and God has done? Here is a
question with broad implications for the Church's public witness.
However we attempt to answer it in the particular contexts of the social
challenges we face, our self-understanding as Christ's Church ought to
start with Christ and bear on our social and political praxis through the
lens of Christian witness, rather than starting with our social and political aspirations and assuming faithful witness will follow automatically
whenever those aspirations are expressed in the name of Christ and his
Church.

This latter impulse has all too often failed us, as have the Caesars of
history and of our own time when we have sought their blessing. And
this raises another question: what does it mean to serve a king who
"opposes Caesar," as we are reminded in St. John's Passion?

Pressures to bow to Caesar, in any case, have existed ever since our
true King was crucified for opposing him, and have in different times
and places taken the form of both persecution and privilege. In the latter case especially, the pressure is often more subtle than the threat of
being thrown to the lions. But it's when we ourselves are in a position
to be tempted to throw others to the lions that the Church is in serious
trouble.

When we insist on the Church's freedom of conscience, we may often have a fine line to walk between two nonetheless polar extremes:
the individualism of liberal society (which in the United States is the
normative paradigm in which we have learned to invoke rights) and the
power-craving nostalgia for the confessional state (which sometimes
underlies the Catholic impulse that chafes against the loss of ecclesial

social privilege).[2] My Anabaptist ancestry compels me—no less so now as a Catholic—to seek a third way, arising in large part from an inherited identity fundamentally shaped by the long memory of having been on the wrong end of state power. For the Mennonite tradition that formed me, given its history, freedom of conscience is vitally important, but in a way that remains both profoundly illiberal and profoundly anti-statist: a strongly communitarian bent (which Catholics certainly share) prevents the insistence on religious freedom from being reduced to merely *individual* conscience, and our historical memory in relation to the state still leaves us with a deep suspicion even of the privileges it may offer.

If I appear to speak somewhat from two traditions at once, it is because I speak as what I am—from a particular combination of the inherited and the chosen, as faith generally is—and because I deeply believe these traditions have much to say to each other. I am focusing here on one particular insight that a Mennonite-informed perspective can offer within the Catholic tradition I have chosen to belong to, although admittedly that legacy is not entirely without ambivalence. An ecclesiology too singly dependent on persecution and martyrdom leaves Mennonites oddly unmoored in their absence—a disorientation the early Anabaptists, with their belief in persecution as the mark of the true church and in the imminence of the eschaton, could not have imagined. Yet their descendants, ironically, now find themselves on essentially equal footing (in relation to the modern American state) with Catholics, who struggle with the opposite disorientation of no longer being the dominant voice in the public square. This strange convergence, while against the grain of deep-seated historical impulses in both directions, demonstrates the need for a third option—one that romanticizes neither persecution nor dominance as an ideal basis for ecclesial identity.

What this will mean for modern-day Mennonites is a question for another discussion, but as Catholics, we may need to rethink some of

---

2  "Liberal" is of course meant here in the broader sense, referring to a widespread consensus on the primacy of individual autonomy on both sides of the U.S. political spectrum.

our expectations vis-à-vis society at large. If the gospel we proclaim is countercultural, which at times it must be, we should certainly still hope and pray for that gospel to take root—but at the same time, we cannot become dependent on the active blessing (or financing!) of the state in order to proclaim it. Indeed, to ensure that what we proclaim is truly gospel may require reexamining the assumption that society would automatically be better off with the Church in power. In order for that to be the case, we must first be oriented in all things toward the example of Christ our head—which, paradoxically, means not seeking a position of power, but rather emptying ourselves, taking the form of a slave.

Our Lord who set us this example also told us that we are blessed when we are hated for his sake. This doesn't mean we should seek out persecution in a masochistic sort of way or hope for our gospel message to be scorned, but it nevertheless means that when scorn does come our way, we can see it not as a foe to be fought but a gift to be received with joy. If social disenfranchisement is the Church's cross, it is an opportunity to imitate our Lord.

Of course, after the kenosis of the cross comes the triumph of the resurrection—and this too is subversive. Praise of the triumphant Lamb means that nothing and nobody in the entire universe has a higher claim on us. We proclaim this subversive ortho-*doxy*—not only right belief, but right praise—every time we sing, "For you *alone* are the holy one, you *alone* are the Lord, you *alone* are the most high, Jesus Christ."

The interrelation of Christ's humility and exaltation is perfectly captured in that great Philippian hymn. Because he humbled himself so radically, his name is above every other name—including the Caesar so threatened by his kingship. The fullness of this duality must be our example. Christ himself, who alone of all humanity was equal to God, has been exalted *because of* his extreme humility and obedience. So we, all the more, cannot attempt to imitate Christ's lordship without first imitating his humility.

 Julia Smucker is a Mennonite by background, a Catholic by choice, and a bridger of dichotomies by necessity. She plies her trade in words as a freelance writer and full-time language service professional.

# Russia and the Rightful Place of the Church

## Uprooting Anna Karenina

The rightful place for the Church, from the contemporary Western perspective, is, well, it has no rightful place. The Church's place has been taken by various abstract nouns (freedom, rights, progress); and what is more, as the legal scholar Kristine Kalanges put it in a recent lecture, today there is "no God but the state."

So far so obvious.

A great deal of truly first-rate material has already been written on the subject of modernity/liberalism, so much so that there is probably no need to dwell on the subject here. We already know, from David L. Schindler and David C. Schindler, Jr. (and other authors of the *Communio* school), from John Milbank, Patrick Deneen, Pierre Manent, and Alisdair MacIntyre, among others, that the historical task of modernity/ liberalism is to uproot the Church and cast it out of the body politic. This will come as a surprise to a reader unfamiliar with this literature, since the Church(es), after all, can still engage in the private practice of worship, and the individual conscience, at least for the moment, is not continuously monitored by the NSA. But the latter response, rather than being a proof of the strong situation of the Church in the modern world, to the contrary, demonstrates the very absence that I am calling attention to, because the rightful place of the Church is pretty much everywhere. Not as an institutional structure, at least, not necessarily. The spirit and ethos of the Church, if it is alive, defines actions from within, in the same way that love defines from within every action of a loving father or mother or spouse. If the ethos is absent, if it is replaced by the spirit of money, or of indifference to all goods but those I define for myself,[1] then the Church itself has not one inch upon which it can build and will disappear.

Events in the news over the past year or so have forced into the limelight the fate of a peculiar part of today's world, a part which, unlike the United States, was not born (or, in the case of much of western Europe, "born again") in the spirit of the Enlightenment. I am speaking of Russia mainly, because it is the culture I know best, but not Russia exclusively. The Slavic world is more than a linguistic category after all, and Eastern Orthodoxy is much more than just the Slavs. For present purposes I will refer to the two together as the East.

Now what strikes me as I consider the recent, often violent, interactions between West and East is that the logic of that confrontation once again is a logic of uprooting. A space that has not yet been quite domi-

---

[1] An elaboration of this thesis can be found in Pierre Manent, *The City of Man* (Princeton: Princeton University Press, 1998), 180: "Why should I not abandon or at least treat lightly what my neighbor, my equal, has the right to dismiss? Each one's right to pursue his good becomes the right … not to seek it." Elsewhere in the same volume can be found a most laconic statement regarding how modernity uprooted the entire world: "Hobbes emphatic concentration of man's nature in the desire for power liberated the world of ideas from every natural attachment and ontological bond. Neither nature nor Being will ever take hold of them again…." (120). As the philosopher Adrian Walker has pointed out in a variety of articles in the journal Communio, as well as in private conversations, it is emphatically *not* the case that modernity/liberalism actually succeeds in its project: it may flee nature and Being, it may laugh mockingly at "the good" (and the Church) but it does not leave the good behind, and perhaps simply cannot do so. One is left with the impression that the real project of modernity is the fragmentation and trivialization, but never the final or simple *destruction* of the good.

nated by the logic of the Enlightenment—and which, to be sure, has yet to find an entirely convincing domestic response to it—is being asked to get with the program of modernization. Which means privatizing the logic and ethos of Orthodoxy (if we are talking about Russia or Eastern Ukraine or Georgia …) and of Catholicism (if we are talking about Poland or Western Ukraine), and getting on with the real business of life as defined by markets, consumer choices and the state (or the E.U., which, to be fair, is more effective than European states taken individually at uprooting everything in sight).

I would like to focus, in what follows, on what is at risk in this uprooting of the Slavic and Orthodox worlds—at risk, that is, from the perspective of those of us concerned with the ethos and logic of the Church. These notes will be impressionistic and unsystematic, perhaps necessarily so.

## What's Love Got to Do with It?

Here's a possible objection to what I have written thus far: "You say that the spirit of the Church is analogous to love in the life of the family. Let us, for the sake of argument, accept your claim. What of it? Loving relationships are just as real and solid outside of your *spirit of the Church*. The Church adds precisely nothing."

To answer this objection I would like to take a look at the Russian novel *Anna Karenina*.

I will begin by emphasizing that it is the novel itself that interests me here, not Tolstoy the man. I am not trying to be fashionably postmodern, divorcing Tolstoy as author from the words he happened to assemble on the page. I respect the intimate connection between the author and his creation. But *Anna Karenina* is something greater than Tolstoy, precisely because it is a work of genius. Such a book can only be written by someone who while writing allowed himself to be open to something of the eternal, something that is clearly beyond this world. To me, *Anna Karenina* has the same status that *The Brothers Karamazov* has for the Dostoevsky scholar Olga Meerson: it is a sort of continuation of the Gospels, or at any rate of what we in the Orthodox world refer to as Sacred Tradition. It is a thoroughly modern addition to that Tradition, while at the same time being a work of art rooted in eternal truths about human nature. Finally, if I may borrow another word from the Orthodox armory, *Anna Karenina,* as a true "icon" of the family and marriage, opens a window for us onto the beauty and tragic seriousness of the very form of love. The family is only one of those forms. But all love (and in essence every icon) takes the form of Christ on the cross.

What is it that uproots marriage and the family? Modernity itself, by making it into merely a choice, something that I myself *create* as opposed to something already given by God. For the Orthodox and Christian Platonic world of the East, marriage is something *given,* and in two senses: first, it is given by nature, just as *eros* is given by nature; but then marriage is made fully itself by the sacred form of marriage which comes into this world from above.

It is necessary to review these rather elementary points because, from the perspective of the modern ethos, it is easy to completely miss what the novel *Anna Karenina* is pointing to. This was made starkly evident not long ago after the film version of the novel, starring Keira Knightly, came out on the big screen, followed by a flood of reviews and comments in magazines and newspapers. Those viewing the movie/novel from a modern perspective inevitably read it as being about a woman in love made to suffer needlessly because of the repressive structure of the time in which she lived, which still labored under the burdens of Tradition. It is a novel about the unhappiness of a woman who should have been happy, and would have been happy had she been fortunate enough to live in our world.

This commonplace perspective does not get everything wrong. The modern reader has every reason to sympathize with the heroine. Indeed, in Anna, Tolstoy has created a modern woman who deserves admiration and sympathy, and with whom, one suspects, the author, despite himself, fell in love. The novel does not moralize at Anna Karenina.

This is what the modern reader so often misses, and it is also something that the most recent film version, while not omitting, deemphasizes: namely, that it is Anna herself who feels from within the spiritual crisis created by her violation of marriage. The violation of marriage causes Anna to suffer not only because of the hypocritical punishment meted out to her by high society, but also, and more importantly, because of something objective and given in what marriage itself is. The official preview of the film promises viewers a love story, and shows a rapturous Anna responding to the sexual consummation of her affair with the words "So this is love!" (The movie itself has Anna using words closer to the original, but they are completely negated by her affect, which is still triumphant.)

The book differs rather starkly from the modernized version. Far from being in raptures when she pronounces the words "Oh God, forgive me!" she is sobbing uncontrollably. A few sentences later we read the following:

> Shame at her spiritual nakedness crushed her and infected him. But in spite of the murderer's horror before the body of his victim, that body must be hacked to pieces and hidden, and the murderer must make use of what he has obtained by his crime.
>
> And, as with fury and passion the murderer throws himself upon the body and drags it and hacks at it, so he covered her face and shoulders with kisses.

Anna accepts his kisses as something that has been purchased by her shame, and she refers to her lover Vronsky as her "accomplice."

## Not Will, But Gift and Givenness

Why does Anna experience the violation of marriage as a shameful degradation, as something comparable to murder? Is it because Tolstoy himself is being too harsh on Anna; or perhaps because Anna has "internalized" the "repressive ethic" of her backward time? And in any case, how could any woman in her right mind choose to stay with Alexei Karenin?

It is time to flesh out a bit the point, stated earlier, that it is Anna herself who considers her marriage sacred. Of course one may counter that Anna is after all simply Tolstoy's creation, but (such is my claim), his "creation" itself has an objective givenness to it. Anna is just as real as you or me. She is what a Russian woman can be, what a Russian— no, what every woman—still is today, at least, in a certain heroic and teleological dimension of the word "woman." But here is the crucial point. It is precisely Anna's inner conviction of the family's sacredness that obliges her to become divided, in her own psyche, against herself, as soon as she allows herself to become infatuated with Vronsky. From that point on she deceives herself at every turn—for example, when she tells herself that Vronsky is not important to her after he already clearly is.

In order for Anna to hide herself from herself she splits her psyche in two. The more superficial and false part of Anna's psyche now sees the world differently. She sees through people and notices all their flaws when formerly they had not been visible. Though formerly she had been open with Karenin ("she always immediately told him all her joys, pleasures and sorrows"), now she marvels at the ease with which she lies to him. Tolstoy uses religiously-tinged language to describe how she accomplishes these deceptions, which infect also her husband: she is seized by "the spirit of evil and deceit."

Now, to stay with Karenin, especially after falling in love with Vronsky, could only have been a cross for Anna. To be sure, in Vronsky at first we confront a shallow dandy with little more than good looks and too much self-confidence. But over time he becomes someone far more substantial. He is patient, courageous, talented, and has in his own way a strong sense of honor. There would have been nothing trivial in giving up Vronsky. Meanwhile, the novel makes clear that, whatever initial respect Anna had for her husband ("He's a good man; upright, kind and remarkable in his own line," Anna says to herself early in the novel), she was unlikely to ever experience with him anything like romantic fulfillment. He was essentially a cultured but boring bureaucrat with a habit of talking ironically even when he meant to be sincere.

Anna deserved someone more like Vronsky. But *Anna Karenina* is not about the travails of a woman who should have been happy. The non-moralizing genius of this novel-icon must be sought elsewhere: in the revelation of the givenness of form of marriage and the family; in the revelation that the form given to marital love, *if that love is accepted in its full seriousness,* is the cross. No one can say that Anna "should" have borne her cross, in other words, that she should have stayed with Karenin. Who among us wants to carry our cross? It is impossible, as Simone Weil has written, for anyone to accept the cross as an act of *will.*

It can only be a matter of grace, something we can perhaps attempt to demand of ourselves, but which we can only receive by asking for it as a gift from somewhere else. It is this sacrificial quality inherent in the given form of marriage which gives to married love its *seriousness*, the seriousness revealed to us in such striking form in the novel *Anna Karenina*.[2] Wherever that sacrificial givenness is present, there too is present the Church—in other words, the form of Christ on the cross. It does not bring us happiness. It brings something quite different. It brings joy and beauty, the beauty that will save the world.

My reference just now to the oft-quoted phrase ("beauty will save the world") from Dostoevsky's *The Idiot* already suggests the wider cultural significance of the single example we have just briefly reviewed. As the Russian philosopher Nikolai Berdyaev affirmed, "[E]verything that was and is original, creative, and significant in our culture, in our literature and philosophy, in our self-awareness—all of it is religious: in its topic, in its aspirations, in its scale." But the religion that forms the background and backbone of this culture is Eastern Orthodox Christianity.[3]

But of course the West knows better and will teach Russia, teach all of us, to reject these dated notions and embrace marriage as something we fashion as we wish. As Weil noted: "Whoever is uprooted himself uproots others."[4]

---

2  I am grateful to my wife Svetlana Grenier, who teaches Russian literature at Georgetown University, for reminding me that the crowns which are held over the heads of the bride and groom during the Orthodox wedding service (called "the crowning") are explicitly associated, in its prayers, with the crowns of martyrs.

3  Prof. Grenier's writings, and our frequent conversations about Russian literature, have, of course, deeply influenced my views on this subject. My own interest in literature, however, is as a source of philosophical anthropology. In any case, any errors of interpretation or other literary sins this essay may contain are entirely my own. I am grateful also to Dr. Olga Meerson of Georgetown University for pointing out this quote from Nicholas Berdyaev.

4  Simone Weil, *The Need for Roots* (London: Routledge, 2002), 48.

Paul Grenier is a writer, translator, and urbanist based in Kensington, Maryland. His written works, mainly essays, span a variety of themes, and include "Terror, Torture and Human Solidarity" (solidarityhall.com) and "The Liturgy of the City" (published in *Second Spring*). He has also translated a number of scholarly works from Russian into English.

# Epilogue

## The Pilgrim and the Radical Approach

It has been said that the collective myths of the modern world are three: *happiness, progress, and technology.*[1] *Happiness,* because the modern man spends his whole life seeking an earthly heaven; *Progress,* because he believes this terrestrial paradise is to be found, not in some historical Eden, but in a future utopia; *Technology,* because he prefers to depend almost exclusively on the material world for the means to realize his chimera.

Any person or group which denies these myths, or interprets the events of life by a different frame of reference, is automatically suspect and ultimately alienated; they find that their society not only fails to provide answers to their most sought-after questions, but that it goes so far as to deny the validity of the questions themselves. Not only are the great mysteries of life unanswerable—but such questions apparently should not even be asked. It is at this point that the truth of this mythology becomes evident: it is a metaphysic of negative space. It does not offer principles on which to build—it creates a vacuum.

---

[1]  Jacques Ellul, *The Technological Society.*

This expulsion of all positive content is felt in all areas: science is nothing but materialism; life is nothing but physiochemical interaction; will is nothing but instinct; social life is nothing but self-interest; economics is nothing but profit-seeking; knowledge itself ends in being nothing but a sophisticated nihilism.

In reading the essays contained in this collection, which it has been my pleasure to prepare for publication, it became obvious to me that there was a single shared question, or perhaps a collective realization, expressed by each of these thoughtful writers, and it was this: What does one do with the negative space—the cultural void—in which we find ourselves?

And their solution? In brief, it was the same solution adopted by Chesterton as he searched for sanity and stability amidst an environment of mental and spiritual chaos. The answer was what he called *orthodoxy*, saying: "I am becoming orthodox because I have come, rightly or wrongly, after stretching my brain till it bursts, to the old belief that heresy is worse even than sin. An error is more menacing than a crime, for an error begets crimes…."[2]

Each of the writers in this collection have met face-to-face the ghastly negative space left by the mythology of the modern world. This remains true even if they have frequently chosen to speak of it using a slightly more specific term: They have spoken instead of *liberalism*. Liberalism is nothing but the most apparent and widely-recognized expression of this self-same mythology, but it is a more appropriate subject for exposition because it is a collection of consciously held ideas, while the underlying myths are elusive and usually unconscious. And so when these writers react in their own unique ways against, among other things, the liberal ideology, they are merely recoiling, in unison, from the darkness of the same void. And apparently, after weathering the storm and surviving the shipwreck, they have all washed up on the same shore discovered by Chesterton.

This is why they have adopted a posture—or perhaps we should call it an *approach*—which they call *radically Catholic*. Orthodoxy is, in the

---

[2] G. K. Chesterton, "The Diabolist," *Tremendous Trifles*.

end, all that is meant by the notion of one being "radically Catholic"—it means simply to pursue orthodoxy in an age in which orthodoxy is considered, at the very least, strange and intransigent, or, at worst, downright idiotic.

So much for the radicalism of these diverse pilgrims—and such men and women *are* pilgrims, regardless of the particular circumstances, experiences, and destinations of each. But their pilgrimage is not one of distance but of reconstruction; their destination is qualitative. They don't need to leave their community to reach their goal; their community *is* their goal. They don't have to leave their neighbors; their objective is to encounter their neighbors—to know them authentically. They don't need to kneel before a relic housed in a distant shrine—although, no doubt, most of them would relish such an opportunity—they instead wish to cultivate the religious ambience of their own immediate surroundings in such a way that their own locality could take on the guise of the shrine, and so that their familiar church altars might assume the aura of the relic.

## Francis as the Vector and Personification of the Pilgrimage

From what has just been said, it is easy to see that this book has a reactionary character: every essay within it is a specific reaction to a contemporary problem, or, as Chesterton said, to a contemporary heresy. But St. Augustine, when he attacked Pelagius, far from merely arguing *against* some crime, was primarily arguing *for* some positive truth. Likewise, these authors cannot in any way be dismissed as mere grouches, ready to offer criticism and nothing else. If they begin from a negative stance, it is because they seek to build something positive.

The variety of ways in which each writer has *reacted* might best illustrate their *radicalism*—which is the first term in this collection's title. It is what differentiates them from each other and from their surroundings. But what unites them? For this, naturally, we may turn to the second term of our title, which is a name: *Francis*. This name, in both its historical connection and in the person of the pontiff who recently adopted it, serves perfectly as the locus of solidarity for all who today would call themselves *radically Catholic*.

Each writer differs in subject matter and method of exposition, but they converge in that they share this same direction. We might say that they address their problems according to a common vector: and that vector is exemplified in the person of Pope Francis.

Some have said that Pope Francis is the first "post-modern" pope. This might be true, but I think that if we agree with this we also need to clarify that this does not necessarily imply that there ever was a "modern" pope. There were pre-modern popes—popes ignored or derided because they were "behind the times"—but there seems never to have been a pope that was truly "with" the times, if we are speaking specifically of the modern period. Even men so congenial to our culture and well-represented in the media as Pope Saint John Paul II were not by any means modernists in either philosophy or habit.

And then we come to Pope Francis. What's the difference?

Some would claim to see here a "discontinuity" of sorts, and I would answer both "yes" and "no." No, if we mean a discontinuity in the Tradition of the Church; yes, if we simply mean that a profound shift has occurred with respect to what I will call the "papal-historical synchronization." What I mean is this: I do not believe that the color or character of the papacy has been profoundly modified between one pontiff and the next in recent history. What has changed, however, is that there has appeared a gradually widening gap between the approach of the papacy and the specific cultural-historical conditions with which it is always forced to contend.

The perpetual mission of the Church is to continuously re-adapt itself, not in *essence* or *nature*, but in *form*, in such a way that it is able to effectively encounter man as he is, ministering to him even while his historical situation shifts beneath his feet. If a crevice opens up amidst the convulsions of history, the Church's job is to be there, snatching civilization from the abyss and leading it back to the Light. In recent history, the ground has shifted with such speed—with such violence—that the Church, true as it may be, has perhaps had difficulty holding onto man amidst the quake; and likewise man himself has struggled to remain intimate with his Church. Man and his eternal missionary have been thrown apart and at a distance that perhaps has not occurred in millennia.

But there has now been something of a shock, felt by millions both within and without the Church, and this shock has been the ascendancy of Pope Francis. From what has been said above it should be clear that this shock is not the result of any discontinuity in the essence of the Church—the shock has been more akin to that felt by a man walking through an alien nation, who has all but given up on hearing anything but babble around him, but who suddenly hears a voice, loud and clear, bellowing from a hilltop: and *lo and behold, he understands the voice.* It speaks to him and it communicates something! It is the shock of being spoken to at a completely unexpected place and time, and from an unexpected direction.

That surprise communication is the personality and message of Pope Francis. It is not that no one was speaking before him; it is not that Benedict XVI did not teach what Francis teaches. It is simply that Francis, following the tradition of the name he has taken, has changed, not the essence of the message, but its tone, dialect, and presentation. Francis feels the void into which he must reach—he knows the materialism, nihilism, and skepticism from which he must reclaim men's minds. Thus, he does not emphasize morality so much as compassion, and he is ready at every moment to mingle acts of mercy with calls for justice. He does not fear paradox. He is capable of writing theology, but he prefers a gospel of *encounter.* He does not lead with condemnation; he leads with the caress. He affirms neither Right nor Left, neither socialist nor capitalist. He moves through such mental barricades as if they were not even there, declaring openly the hollowness of ideology:

> ... ideology does not beckon [people]. In ideologies there is not Jesus: in his tenderness, his love, his meekness. And ideologies are rigid, always. Of every sign: rigid. And when a Christian becomes a disciple of the ideology, he has lost the faith: he is no longer a disciple of Jesus, he is a disciple of this attitude of thought.... For this reason Jesus said to them: "You have taken away the key of knowledge."

In short, he faces the *negative space* before him not by attempting to preach into it (for sound does not carry within a vacuum), but by inserting himself into the cold and the dark, ready to meet men where they are.

And everyone has felt him, judging from the wide array of reactions flowing in from all quarters. He has succeeded, then, with his *encounter*—it was the jolt mentioned above, and the collision has proven a bit more violent than many of us were prepared to endure. It was as if a massive gear suddenly locked back into place at the center of a machine which had long lay inert. The great gear is the Church; the groove is in the heart of the world; and the torque between the two—that pressure for motion which, through Francis, has disconcerted so many—is proof of the life of the Holy Spirit.

Whatever one's opinion of the pontiff, he is moving things—minds and mouths, at least, if not hearts as well—in a way that we have not seen in some time. The prayer of this book is that we may augment his cause as he rouses so many from sleep. And our hope is that we may join in the awakening.

Daniel Schwindt is editor-in-chief at Solidarity Hall. He and his wife live in central Kansas, a cultural navel of the world from which he has produced a series of non-fiction collections: *Letter to my Generation: On Identity, Direction, and Disbelief; The Pursuit of Sanity;* and *Holocaust of the Childlike.*

### SOLIDARITY HALL

# Come Join Us in the Hall!

Solidarity Hall is going places.

First, we're going into book publishing—as Solidarity Hall Press—and, second, into offering Solidarity Hall memberships, along with which there will be conferences and opportunities to attend meetups with fellow Solidarians. (If that's the word we want.)

For two years or so, our writers and editors have been posting and publishing on the roots of community and the sources of community renewal, drawing on the inspiration of several tribal elders in this area: G. K. Chesterton, Jane Jacobs, E. F. Schumacher, Dorothy Day, Ivan Illich, Wendell Berry. (We call them our "presiding spirits.")

Thus we've been a kind of oasis for people searching for the intersection of traditional wisdom and the New Economy. And now we're moving toward something bigger.

We're launching Solidarity Hall Press, a program to publish in both e-book and print versions, beginning with:

### *Radically Catholic in the Age of Francis*

Edited by Daniel Schwindt, this collection of personal essays gives a glimpse into the hopes and expectations of some two dozen men and women—not all Catholics—attempting to live in a more radically Catholic fashion, partly inspired by the teachings and example of Pope Francis and his predecessors.

## Ancestral Voices for the Commons

Edited by Susannah Black, these essays pay tribute to a group of seminal communitarian thinkers, each of whom has left a legacy of reflection desperately needed today. Subjects here include G. K. Chesterton, Wendell Berry, Dorothy Day, Jane Jacobs, E. F. Schumacher, Simone Weil, and others. An interesting extension of this title might be a series of podcasts which are interviews with the authors of each piece about their subjects. These could lay the groundwork for a regular series of S.H. podcasts aimed at crunchy communitarians of various flavors.

## New Rules for Radicals

Saul Alinsky was an interesting chap but his rules were for an earlier, arguably far too narrowly political, time. Going beyond politics to the power of local association, New Rules for Radicals is a handbook for the new community organizer, focused on community wealth-building and healing, neighborhood by neighborhood. It's not about controlling the government: it's about finding each other.

Want to keep in touch? Just sign up for our mailing list (drop us a note at info@solidarityhall.org) and you'll be in the loop.

Made in the USA
Lexington, KY
30 June 2015